Producing Music
with Digital Performer

Ben Newhouse

Berklee Media

Vice President: Dave Kusek
Dean of Continuing Education: Debbie Cavalier
Business Manager: Linda Chady Chase
Technology Manager: Mike Serio
Marketing Manager, Berkleemusic: Barry Kelly
Senior Graphic Designer: David Ehlers

Berklee Press

Senior Writer/Editor: Jonathan Feist
Writer/Editor: Susan Gedutis Lindsay
Production Manager: Shawn Girsberger
Marketing Manager, Berklee Press: Jennifer Rassler
Product Marketing Manager: David Goldberg
Production Assistant: Louis Ochoa

ISBN 0-87639-056-4

1140 Boylston Street
Boston, MA 02215-3693 USA
(617) 747-2146

Visit Berklee Press Online at
www.berkleepress.com

DISTRIBUTED BY

HAL•LEONARD®
CORPORATION
7777 W. BLUEMOUND RD. P.O. BOX 13819
MILWAUKEE, WISCONSIN 53213

Visit Hal Leonard Online at
www.halleonard.com

Printed in the United States of America by Vicks Lithograph and Printing Corporation

11 10 09 08 07 06 05   5 4 3 2

Contents

CD Audio Tracks and Project Files vi

Preface. vii

Acknowledgments. viii

1 Hardware Setup 1
1.1 Installing Digital Performer 1
1.2 What is MIDI? 1
1.3 MIDI Connections 2
1.4 Using MIDI with Digital Performer 3
1.5 Audio MIDI Setup 4
1.6 Incorporating a Mixing Board 5
1.7 Incorporating an Audio Interface 6
1.8 Incorporating a Microphone 7
1.9 Complete Setup 8
1.10 Signal Flow and Troubleshooting 9
1.11 Smaller Studios. 9
1.12 Software Sound Sources. 11

2 The Basics 12
2.1 The Project Folder 12
2.2 Launching Digital Performer 13
2.3 The Digital Performer Environment 14
2.4 Saving Your File 15
2.5 Templates 15
2.6 Multiple Sequences. 16

3 Navigation Tools 18
3.1 The Control Panel 18
3.2 Playback Control. 18
3.3 Counters 19
3.4 Tempo Indicator. 20
3.5 Metronome, Countoff, and Wait Features. 21
3.6 Memory Cycle. 22
3.7 Control Panel Drawers 23

4 Sequence Editor. 24
4.1 The Sequence Editor 24
4.2 Title Bar Buttons 24
4.3 Track Types. 25
4.4 Track Information Panel 26
        Audio Track Information 27
        MIDI Track Information. 29
4.5 Tracks Overview 29
4.6 Manipulating Tracks. 31
4.7 Sequence Editor Example Layouts 34

5 File Setup 37
5.1 "Upbeat Rock" Example 37
5.2 Create Appropriate Tracks 42
5.3 Name Tracks 45
5.4 Assign Appropriate Outputs 46
        Studios with Mixing Boards 47
        Studios without Mixing Boards 48
5.5 Assign Patches 52
5.6 Set Tempo 53
        Conductor Track versus Tempo Slider 53
        Changing the Conductor Track 54
        Changing the Tempo Slider 57
        Conductor Track versus
        Tempo Slider Conclusion. 57
        Additional Conductor Track Data 58
5.7 Sequence Start Time 59
5.8 Markers 60
5.9 Review. 62

6 Recording MIDI 63
6.1 Record Enable. 63
6.2 Recording MIDI 64
        Bass Drum. 64

Snare Drum 65
Remaining Drums 65
Bass, Keyboards, and Brass 66

6.3 Additional Recording Techniques 67
Overdub 67
Punch-In 67

6.4 What If I Don't Play Keyboards? 68
Step Record 68
Drawing Notes 68
Using Your Keyboard 69

7 Editing Your MIDI Performance 70
7.1 Tools Palette 70
7.2 Deleting and Moving Notes 71
7.3 Event Information Bar 73
7.4 Changing Start and End Points 74
7.5 Scissors 75
7.6 Velocity Layer 76
7.7 Additional Selection Techniques 78
Cross-Hair Pointer 78
Double-Clicking on Data 79
Double-Clicking on the Keyboard Icon 79
Lasso 80
I-Beam 81
Time Ruler Selecting 82
Selection Drawer 83
Select All 85
Object and Time Range Selections . . . 86
7.8 Copy/Cut/Paste/Merge 87
7.9 Loops 88
7.10 Quantize 90
"Upbeat Rock" Quantized to Eighths . 91
"Upbeat Rock" Quantized
to Half Notes 92
"Upbeat Rock" Quantized
to Swing Eighths 92
Randomize 93

Sensitivity and Strength 94
Groove Quantize 94
Creating Grooves 96
7.11 Change Duration 97
7.12 Transpose 99
7.13 Change Velocity 99
7.14 Undo History 101

8 Editing Windows 103
8.1 Event List 104
8.2 Graphic Editor 105
8.3 Drum Editor 108
8.4 Notation Editor 111
8.5 Quickscribe Editor 113
8.6 Tracks Window 115

9 Recording Audio 117
9.1 Analog and Digital Audio 117
9.2 Sample Rate and Format 117
9.3 Digital Word Clock 120
9.4 Buffer Size 121
9.5 File Management 123
9.6 Audio Monitor Window 124
9.7 Inputs and Outputs 125
9.8 Ready to Record 128
9.9 Other Audio Sources 129
9.10 Audio Voices 130

10 Editing Audio 132
10.1. Soundbites 132
10.2 Audio Track Cursors 133
Arrow 133
Cross-Hair 133
Trimmer 134
Finger 134
I-Beam 135
Scissors 135
10.3 Removing Unwanted Space 136
10.4 Copying and Pasting Audio 138

10.5   Fades   140
      Fade-ins and Fade-outs   140
      Crossfades   143
10.6   Creating a Composite Performance   145
10.7   Non-Destructive Editing   146
10.8   Deleting Unused Audio   147
11   Mixing   149
11.1   Mixing Board Layout   149
11.2   Setting Volumes   150
11.3   Setting Panning   150
11.4   A Basic Mix   151
11.5   Effects   153
      Audio Inserts   153
      MIDI Inserts   156
11.6   Internal Bussing   157
      Using Busses with Effects   158
      Using Busses to Reduce CPU Load . .   159
11.7   Track Groups   161
11.8   Automation Snapshot   163
      Taking the Snapshot   164
      Play-Enabling the Automation   166
11.9   Continuous Controllers   166
11.10 Using Continuous Controllers   168
      Expression Versus Volume   171
11.11 Creating Dynamics on Audio Tracks . . .   172
11.12 Master Fader   173
11.13 Additional Automation   174
      MIDI   174
      Audio   174
12   Musical Considerations   177
12.1   MIDIstration   177
      Simulating a Live Performance   177
12.2   Layering   179

12.3   Audio Processing   180
13   Printing Your Final Mix   183
13.1   Recording Your Mix   183
13.2   Bouncing to Disk   185
13.3   Mastering   189
13.4   Exporting to AIFF   190
13.5   Burning to CD   192
      Burning an Audio CD   193
      Burning a Data CD   194
13.6   Other Delivery Formats   194
14   Writing to Picture   197
14.1   Locking to a Quicktime Movie:
      Importing a Movie   197
14.2   Start Time   199
14.3   Frame Rate   201
14.4   Auxiliary Counter   202
14.5   Using Markers   202
15   Digital Performer Projects   206
15.1   Set Up Your Studio   206
15.2   Creating Tempo Changes   206
15.3   J.S. Bach   207
15.4   Funk Bass and Drums   208
15.5   Creating Dynamics   209
15.6   Poignant Moment   210
15.7   Piano Chase Editing   212
15.8   Knockoff   213
15.9   Audio Editing   213
15.10 Record Vocals   214
15.11 Advanced Audio   214
15.12 One Note   214

      Conclusion   215
      About the Author   216
      Index   217

CD Audio Tracks and Project Files

AUDIO TRACKS		PAGE
1	"Upbeat Rock" Full Band	37
2	All Drums	66
3	Bass, Keyboard, and Brass	66
4	Loop	89
5	Quantized to Eighth Notes	91
6	Quantized to Half Notes	92
7	Quantized to Swing Eighths	92
8	Upbeat Guitar	129
9	Volume Fade	172
10	Automated Panning Curves	174
11	Automated EQ Curves	176
12	Layered Keyboard Sounds	179
13	Processed Audio	181
14	"Minuet in G" by J.S. Bach	207
15	Funk Bass/Drums Groove	208
16	Dramatic Transition using Dynamics	209
17	"Poignant Moment"	210
18	"One Note"	214

PROJECT FILES		
P01	File Setup	61
P02	Drums	66
P03	All MIDI	66
P04	Loops	89
P05	Upbeat Guitar	129
P06	Fade In and Out	143
P07	Crossfades	145
P08	Master fader	173
P09	Embellishment	179
P10	Processed Audio	181
P11	Piano Chase	212
P12	Audio Editing	213
P13	Record Vocals	213
P14	Advanced Audio	214

Preface

Congratulations and welcome! You have joined a vast group of musicians who use Digital Performer, ranging from renowned film composers to amateur musicians. What do they have in common? They all want to compose, record, and produce music on their computer. Digital Performer enables them to do this.

This book and CD will guide you through the process of setting up your equipment and making music with it. It is divided into three primary sections. Chapters 1 to 4 deal with setting up your studio and getting familiar with your computing environment. Chapters 5 to 14 deal with musical issues, discussing the processes of recording, editing, mixing, and mastering. Chapter 15 is a review section, where you will complete hands-on musical projects. The accompanying CD includes examples, both of Digital Performer project files and audio tracks, to illustrate the techniques being executed and the audio being created.

This book is a stand-alone introduction to Digital Performer, and it includes both essential features and advanced techniques. It also serves as the textbook for the Berkleemusic.com online courses on Digital Performer. If you would like to take a more multidimensional approach to learning Digital Performer, these online courses add projects, interaction with a community of other Digital Performer users, guidance from a Berklee professor (sometimes me!), multimedia demonstrations of some techniques, and many other benefits and conveniences of Web instruction. Visit http://www.berkleemusic.com for details.

Now, let's get started.

Acknowledgments

Special Thanks to:

Berklee Press for their vision and commitment, particularly Debbie Cavalier, David Kusek, Jonathan Feist, and Shawn Girsberger; Berklee College of Music for providing an unparalleled learning environment, especially Matthew Nicholl, Jerry Smith, Loudon Stearns, Kevin Michael, Catherine Boger, Mike Carrera, Phil Ruokis, Jeri Sykes, and Sarah Brindell; MOTU for awesome software and hardware, especially Jim Cooper; Alan Ett Music Group for the opportunity to work and learn, particularly Alan Ett, Scott Liggett, Irl Sanders, Ryan Neill, Tim Aarons (fruit thrower), William Ashford, and Jon Schell; Mike Post for his generosity with his time and talents; so many colleagues and friends in the music business, particularly Phil Sheeran, Lois Fein and Dandy, Kenny Golde, Dick Whitaker, Doug Wood, Martha Gibbons, Jim Lum (world's best guitarist), Syd Johnson, and Jim McCarty for fabulous drum tracks; the greatest family on earth for their unconditional love and support; and Stephanie Holmes, for her astounding patience and encouragement.

HARDWARE SETUP

1.1 Installing Digital Performer

When you purchase Digital Performer, you are provided with installation disks, a registration number, and a manual. To install the software, insert the CD into your computer and follow the instructions, filling in your name and registration information when prompted. If you have problems during the installation and registration process, technical support is offered by MOTU at 617-576-3066 (9:00 A.M. to 6:00 P.M. EST, Monday through Friday). Additional information regarding MOTU products can be found at www.motu.com.

Setting up your studio can be a daunting task. Most likely, you have more than just your computer to deal with. You may have multiple MIDI and audio hardware devices, and possibly several software programs. The rest of this chapter details how to connect all the essential hardware necessary for a small- to medium-sized Digital Performer studio.

1.2 What is MIDI?

MIDI (Musical Instrument Digital Interface) is a standard protocol that allows individual musical instruments to communicate information with each other about a musical performance. MIDI hardware has three types of cable ports: MIDI In, MIDI Out, and MIDI Thru, through which MIDI messages are sent to and from other devices. Not all devices have all three types of ports.

MIDI messages most commonly are generated by a keyboard or computer. It is important to understand that these messages don't contain actual audio. Rather, they include raw computer data that later will be interpreted to create audio. The most common MIDI message is the Note On message. When you play a note on a MIDI keyboard, a Note On message is generated. This message contains all the information regarding what you just did—namely, what note you played (Note Name) and how hard you played it (On Velocity). This information is sent through the keyboard's MIDI Out port and travels over a MIDI cable to a sound module.

The sound module, in turn, creates audio based on the incoming messages. The MIDI message's "Note Name" parameter determines the pitch generated by the sound module, and the "On Velocity" determines the timbre and loudness of the audio generated.

A MIDI performance is nothing more than a sequence of these MIDI messages. In its simplest form, it is a sequence of Note On and Note Off messages. Of course, these performances can get quite complex, incorporating pitch bend, volume changes, and much more.

Any hardware device or software program, such as Digital Performer, that allows you to record and playback these messages is called a "sequencer." Once recorded, you can refine the sequenced performance, changing notes, changing speeds, altering articulations, adding layers, and more. Once you have perfected your work of art, you can send this performance to a sound module that converts it into genuine, bona fide audio. In this manner, you can get the *exact* performance you desire.

Digital Performer allows you to store and edit MIDI messages, in order to create musical performances, and this is one of its most powerful uses.

1.3 MIDI Connections

Let's make a very simple MIDI connection between a MIDI controller and sound module, which will be much like the kind of connections that you will make in your own Digital Performer studio setup.

A *MIDI controller* is an instrument you play to generate the original MIDI message. The most common type of MIDI controller is a keyboard, but there are MIDI guitars, drums, even trumpets. A *sound module* is a device that inputs (receives) MIDI messages and outputs (plays) the corresponding audio. Sound modules typically store hundreds or thousands of sounds, such as pianos, basses, drums, etc. In Digital Performer, these sounds are referred to as "patches."

MIDI instruments use MIDI In, MIDI Out, and MIDI Thru ports to communicate to other devices. The MIDI In port is used to receive incoming messages. The MIDI Out port is used to send outgoing messages. The MIDI Thru port sends an exact copy of the data received on the MIDI In port to another device.

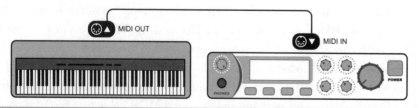

FIGURE 1.1 MIDI Connection from Controller to Sound Module

In figure 1.1, a MIDI controller (such as a Korg Triton) is used to generate MIDI messages. These messages leave the keyboard through its MIDI Out port. They travel over a MIDI cable to the sound module's MIDI In port. The sound module (XV-3080) interprets these messages, generating the appropriate audio. This audio must then be sent to speakers or headphones, in order to be heard.

Some samplers and synthesizers can also play the role of converting MIDI to audio. The sound from a *synthesizer* is entirely computer generated. A *sampler*, on the other hand, uses stored audio files to generate sound. Rather than generating sounds that simulate a trumpet, a sampler replays actual audio recordings of a trumpet.

1.4   Using MIDI with Digital Performer

To utilize MIDI with Digital Performer, these connections must reach your computer. Computers typically communicate with MIDI devices using a USB (Universal Serial Bus), FireWire, or serial cable.

The computer rarely connects directly to a sound module or MIDI controller, but rather to a MIDI interface. A *MIDI Interface* is a hardware device that allows multiple MIDI devices to communicate with one another. The MIDI interface acts like a traffic cop, standing in the intersection between all of the MIDI devices, directing the flow of traffic.

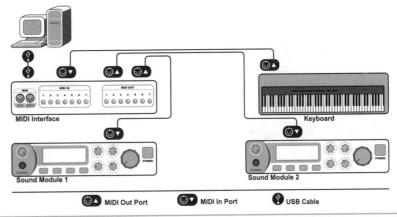

FIGURE 1.2 Setup with MIDI Interface. Includes computer, MIDI controller, MIDI interface, and two sound modules.

Figure 1.2 incorporates a MIDI controller (Roland A-30), a MIDI interface (MOTU Micro Express), two sound modules (Korg Triton Rack and Roland XV-3080), and a computer. When you play a note on the keyboard, a MIDI message is generated and sent to the MIDI interface. The MIDI interface sends it to the computer, where it can be recorded. In Digital Performer, you indicate which sound module you intend to use. It sends this message back to the MIDI interface, and the MIDI interface then sends the message to that destination.

1.5   Audio MIDI Setup

To work properly, the MIDI interface must be told what devices are connected to it and to which ports they are connected. You input this information in your computer using a system utility called Audio MIDI Setup. To create a MIDI setup, select Setup–Open Audio MIDI Setup, or from within the Finder at Applications–Utilities–Audio MIDI Setup. Click on the "MIDI Devices" tab to access your MIDI setup.

When your MIDI Interface is connected to your computer (and turned on…), it will show up in your setup automatically. Next, use the "Add Device" button to add the keyboards and modules to your studio. After a device is added, double-click on its icon to assign it an appropriate manufacturer and model. Last, virtually connect them to your interface by dragging on each instrument icon's "in" and "out" triangles.

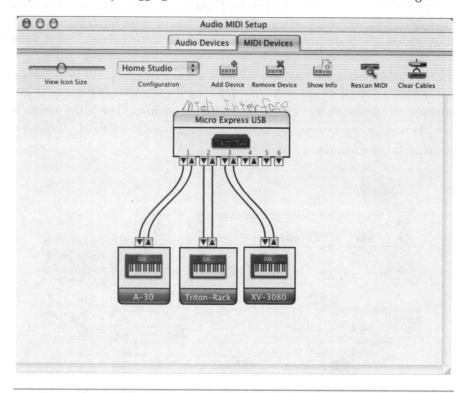

FIGURE 1.3 Audio MIDI Setup: MIDI Devices

Figure 1.3 illustrates the setup necessary for the diagram shown in figure 1.2. The MIDI controller is connected via port 1, the Triton Rack via port 2, and the XV-3080 via port 3. This must reflect *exactly* how the devices are connected in your physical studio.

1.6 Incorporating a Mixing Board

With this basic studio setup, we can generate MIDI signals with a MIDI controller, then record, edit, and replay the MIDI with a computer, convert this MIDI to audio with multiple sound modules, and connect all these devices with a MIDI Interface. This is an admirable start.

However, we do not yet have any way of combining the audio generated by the different sound modules into one signal. We can't hear, say, a drum machine accompanying a separate guitar sound module. Typically, this function of combining audio sources is performed by a mixing board. Though Digital Performer has a virtual mixing board, many users like to have an external one as part of their hardware setup, as well, as it provides added flexibility.

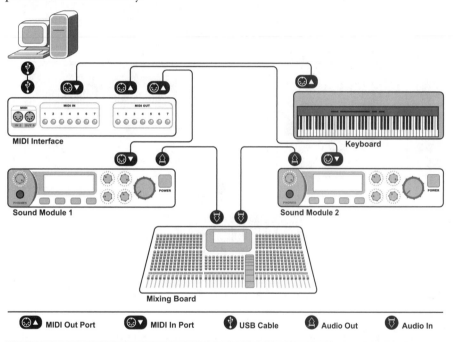

FIGURE 1.4 MIDI Setup with Mixing Board. Includes computer, MIDI controller, MIDI interface, two sound modules, and mixing board.

In figure 1.4, we have added a mixing board to the basic setup. In this scenario, the mixing board receives audio coming from the Triton Rack and the XV-3080. The board combines these signals into one stereo signal, which is sent on to an amplifier/ speakers.

The cables you use to connect your sound sources to your mixing board will depend on whether you are using digital or analog equipment. The most common analog cable for these kinds of transfers is the quarter-inch cable. There are many different kinds of digital cables, including TDIF, ADAT Lightpipe, and S/PDIF.

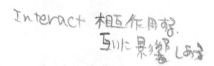

1.7 Incorporating an Audio Interface

At the mixing board, we can combine our various audio signals into one stereo signal. This can be sent to our speakers or headphones for monitoring or to a hardware recorder, such as a DAT player. Of course, you may also wish to send this to your computer and record it onto your hard drive, where you can burn it onto a CD.

To record to your hard drive, you must add an audio interface. An *audio interface* is a hardware device that allows a computer to interact with external audio devices, such as a mixing board, microphone, instrument (such as electric bass), or sound module.

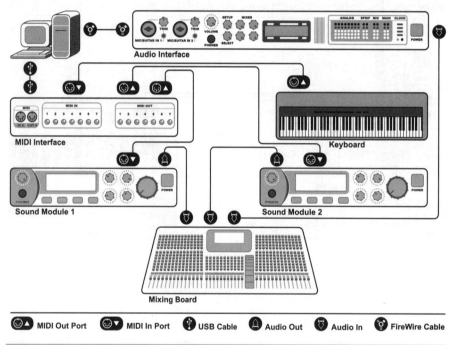

FIGURE 1.5 MIDI Setup with Audio Interface. Includes computer, MIDI controller, MIDI interface, two sound modules, mixing board, and audio interface.

In figure 1.5, we have added an audio interface (MOTU 828 Mark II) to the setup. It is connected to the computer with a FireWire cable. In addition, it is connected to the mixing board. This connection will allow us to send audio between the mixing board and our computer. This audio could be coming from our sound modules, the signal from a microphone, or a combination of both.

In Digital Performer, you must indicate that you would like to use your audio interface, rather than the computer's internal audio system. Choose Setup–Configure Audio System–Configure Hardware Driver to set this.

［電算日（ミステムとして）構成する.

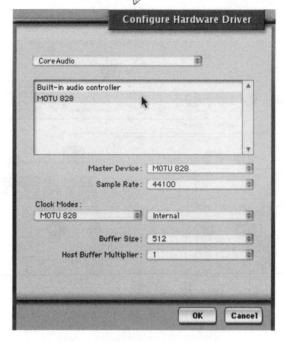

FIGURE 1.6 Configure Hardware Driver Window

Here, you can select what audio hardware you would like to use. In figure 1.6, the user is selecting the MOTU 828 as his audio hardware. After doing so, all audio from Digital Performer will be sent to the 828. The "Built-in audio controller" refers to the built-in speakers on your computer. If you choose this, your audio will sound through your computer's internal speakers. (Settings for audio hardware will be discussed further in chapter 9.)

1.8 Incorporating a Microphone

To record ambient audio, we need a microphone. The signal from a microphone must be run through a preamp before it is recorded on your hard drive, to boost the microphone's signal to a usable level.

Get to know your mixing board and audio interface; it will likely have built-in preamps. The microphone can be connected to the mixing board's preamp and subsequently routed to the audio interface and computer. Or, the microphone could be connected directly to the audio interface. Generally, there is no benefit to one or the other. Experiment with both, and use the one that results in the highest quality recordings.

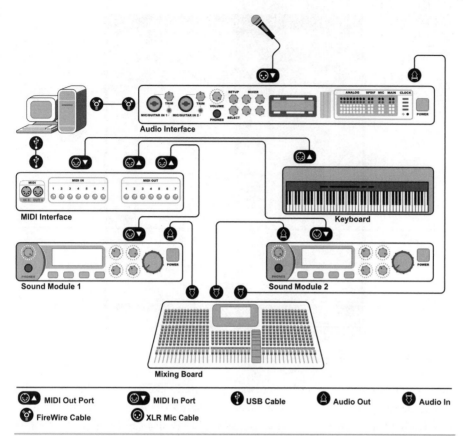

FIGURE 1.7 Mid-Level Setup. Includes computer, MIDI controller, MIDI interface, audio interface, mixing board, two sound modules, and a microphone.

1.9 Complete Setup

At this point, we have created a mid-level studio. It has many powerful capabilities. We can create MIDI performances on our controller, record and edit them in our computer, and trigger external sound modules. We can record live vocals and instrumentals directly onto our hard drive. Once recorded, we can use Digital Performer to edit, revise, transpose, and change speeds of the music, and much more. While the specific gear will vary from studio to studio, this general setup is very typical among composers and sound designers.

It is common to expand this setup by adding additional MIDI sound sources. We could also add additional microphones and preamps to be able to record multiple tracks simultaneously. We could also add external hardware to the mixing board, such as reverb and delay boxes.

1.10 Signal Flow and Troubleshooting

As your setup grows, it becomes increasingly important to understand the signal flow of your studio. *Signal flow* refers to the sequence in which your musical data passes from device to device. In the mid-level setup above, MIDI signals begin at the MIDI controller. They are then sent to the MIDI Interface. The MIDI Interface sends the message to the computer. At the computer, Digital Performer indicates which sound source will be used, and Audio MIDI Setup indicates where this sound source is connected to the MIDI Interface. At this point, the MIDI message will be sent to its final destination: the sound module. Here, the signal is converted into actual audio and sent to the mixing board. At the mixing board, you can choose to send it to the amplifier/speakers or the audio interface.

Why should you care about how the signal flows? Knowing the steps in the chain reaction will help you troubleshoot, when something goes wrong. If you are not getting sound, start at the beginning of your signal flow (probably the keyboard), and work your way through to the end (probably the speakers). Many devices have LED lights on the front indicating whether they are receiving signal. At some point, the lights will stop blinking. This is where the connection has gone awry.

1.11 Smaller Studios

All this gear can cost a lot of money. Luckily, it is getting increasingly easier to begin with a smaller setup. There are many devices that combine the function of more than one piece of hardware. For instance, it is now possible to buy gear that combines the functions of the MIDI and audio interfaces. One such device is MOTU's 828 Mk II.

FIGURE 1.8 MOTU 828 Mk II Audio/MIDI Interface

As you can see in figure 1.8, the Mark II still has a FireWire connection to communicate audio information with the computer. In addition, it has MIDI In and Out ports, allowing it to communicate directly with one MIDI instrument.

In addition, it is common for MIDI keyboards to contain internal sounds, in addition to serving as MIDI controllers. In this case, one device can act as both a MIDI controller and a sound module. One such instrument is the Korg Triton. So, we could start a smaller studio by connecting an 828 to our computer, and a Triton to the 828.

Moreover, it is possible to do without a mixing board, in a small studio. Rather than connecting the audio outs of the keyboard to a mixing board, connect them to the audio inputs of the 828. Here, it can be combined with any other audio you are using, with each element sent through the 828's main outputs.

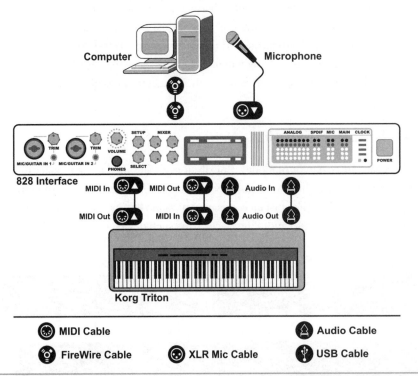

FIGURE 1.9 Introductory Studio. Includes computer, audio/MIDI interface, microphone, and MIDI controller/sound module.

This would be a very powerful introductory studio. It would allow you to record multiple MIDI tracks and convert them to audio. In addition, you could layer live instrumentals and vocals. Using Digital Performer's internal mixing board, you could set appropriate levels and effects. Its primary limitation is the inability to add additional MIDI hardware. Since you have only one MIDI in/out on the 828, you could communicate to and from only one device. For more information on using this setup, see chapter 5.

1.12 Software Sound Sources

Software sound sources (also called "virtual instruments" or "plug-ins") are a great way to expand your studio, particularly if you are beginning with a smaller setup. These programs function like hardware sound modules or samplers; they convert your MIDI performance into actual audio using banks of stored audio files. There are three types of plug-in formats that can interact with Digital Performer:

1. AU (Audio Units)

2. MAS (MOTU Audio System)

3. Rewire

In chapter 5, we will discuss precisely how to set up your file so that DP can interact with these programs.

MIDI Hardware Terminology Reference

This is a brief overview of common MIDI hardware and what function each can play in a Digital Performer setup.

MIDI Controller — A device on which you perform to create the original MIDI signals. Most commonly, a keyboard.

MIDI Interface — A device that allows multiple MIDI instruments and a computer to communicate with one another. The MIDI interface acts like a traffic cop, standing in the intersection between all of the MIDI devices, directing the flow of traffic.

Audio Interface — A device that allows the computer to communicate with external audio devices.

Sound Module — A device that receives MIDI messages and converts them to the corresponding audio. Sound modules typically store hundreds of sounds, such as pianos, basses, and drums.

Sampler — A device that receives MIDI messages and converts them to the corresponding audio. A sampler creates audio by triggering actual audio files (samples) stored in its memory.

Synthesizer — A device that generates and modifies audio electronically.

Sequencer — A hardware or software device that enables the user to record, edit, and play back MIDI events. Digital Performer is a software sequencer. Many keyboards, such as the Korg Triton, have built-in sequencers.

FireWire — A type of cable used to transfer data to and from computers at high speeds. FireWire is currently the most common choice for connecting audio hardware to a computer.

USB — A type of cable and port used to transfer data to and from computers. USB is currently the most common choice for connecting MIDI devices to a computer.

Serial — A type of cable and port used to transfer data to and from computers. Older computers and MIDI interfaces may require a serial connection.

THE BASICS

2.1 The Project Folder

Digital Performer generates multiple files, in the process of creating a music project. These file types include sequence files, audio files, fade files, and others. To keep this information organized, all of these files will be located in one folder: the Project folder. Inside every project folder are subfolders to store each file type, named "Audio Files," "Fades," and so on.

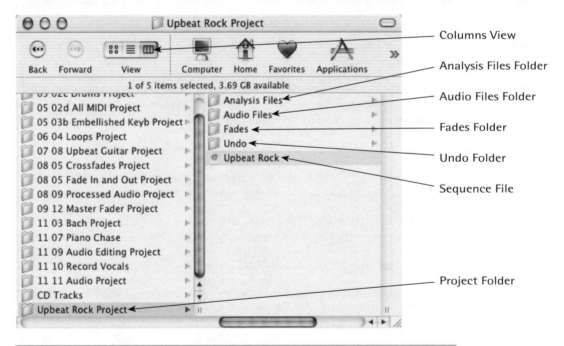

FIGURE 2.1 The Project Folder Layout. This Project folder includes a sequence file, Analysis Files folder, Audio Files folder, Fades folder, and Undo folder.

For the most part, you will not need to be overly concerned about these files and folders. This structure is simply Digital Performer's way of storing and organizing data. There should be virtually no time when you open up the Fades, Analysis, Audio, or Undo folders and move files around. Nearly all tasks related to these files are most safely completed from within Digital Performer.

However, this file structure becomes important when you are copying your project to another drive or CD for backup or storage. When you do so, copying *only* the sequence file is insufficient. If you do so, all other data (including your audio files) will be left behind. To back up, you must copy/move your *entire* project folder, with its structure intact.

2.2 Launching Digital Performer

Like any program, you can start Digital Performer several ways: clicking its icon in the OSX dock, double-clicking on the program icon itself, or double-clicking on a sequence file for a particular project. When double-clicking a particular sequence file, this file will automatically be opened. When opening the program directly, Digital Performer prompts you for which file you would like to open.

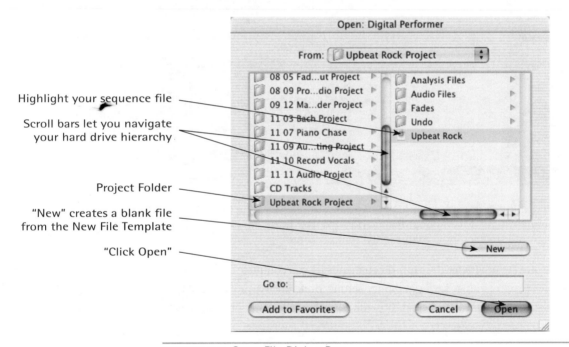

FIGURE 2.2 Open File Dialog Box

To open a preexisting file, locate it on your hard drive, highlight the sequence file, and click "Open." Clicking "New" will create a blank file based on your New File Template (discussed later this chapter). You will then be prompted to name your new project. Give it a name, select a drive location, and click Save. Creating a new project automatically creates a Project folder, Sequence File, and Audio Files folder.

If Digital Performer is already running, you can open a preexisting file (shortcut: Command-o) or create a new file (shortcut: Command-n) from the File menu.

2.3 The Digital Performer Environment

Once you open a file, you will see several windows. Digital Performer has a wide range of windows, each of which accomplishes a specialized task or type of editing. The windows you see when you create a new file will be determined by the properties of your New File Template. The most often-used windows are the Control Panel, Sequence Editor, Mixing Board, and Tools Palette, shown in figure 2.3.

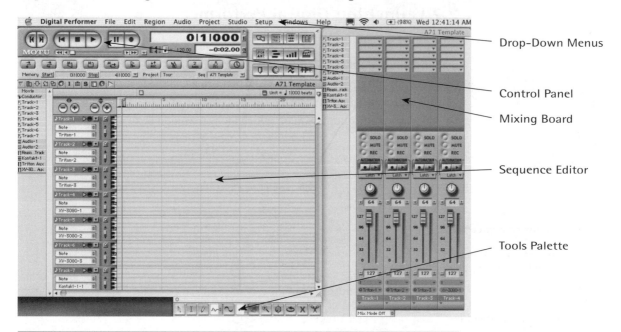

FIGURE 2.3 Digital Performer's Working Environment. Includes the Control Panel, Sequence Editor, Mixing Board, and Tools Palette. These windows may appear differently, depending on your individual settings.

Like many software programs, the drop-down menus let you complete a wide variety of tasks, including opening, saving, editing, setting preferences, and more. Many windows also have mini-menus, which provide easy access to functions relevant to that window.

The Control Panel (shortcut: Shift-x) allows you to navigate your file, with features such as play, stop, record, counter display, and more (see chapter 3).

The Sequence Editor (shortcut: Shift-s) gives you a broad overview of your tracks and allows you to record and edit your performance (see chapter 4).

The Mixing Board (shortcut: Shift-m) allows you to set volumes, panning, effects, and more (see chapter 11).

The Tools Palette provides a variety of cursors that accomplish particular editing and selection tasks (see chapter 7). It may display horizontally or vertically, depending on your preference.

2.4 Saving Your File

Save (shortcut: Command-s) is located in the File Menu. When you save a file, you must give it three properties: file name, drive location, and file format. The file format is typically based on the version of the program you are running, such as Digital Performer 4.1. Notably, a Digital Performer 4.1 file cannot be opened by previous versions of Digital Performer, but previous-version files *can* be opened by Digital Performer 4.1. If you are collaborating, be sure you know what version of the program your co-writer is running before you send him or her a file.

If you saved your file previously, Digital Performer will retain the same file name, drive location, and file format. If you would like to change any of these properties, select "Save As" from the File Menu.

WARNING: While Digital Performer creates a Project Folder when you create a new file, it does not do so when you are utilizing Save As; it instead creates only a new sequence file.

2.5 Templates

You may wish to customize your starting point for projects, in terms of window displays, track types and settings, and other preferences. You can do so by altering your New File Template and creating additional templates. Personally, I find this particularly useful. I prefer to work on a laptop, so that I can bounce around between several studios. Each studio has a different set of hardware. Therefore, I have a different template to act as a starting point at each studio.

To create a template, first create a new file. Set up this file to appear as you would like your workspace to appear when you begin working. Then choose File–Save As Template.

FIGURE 2.4 Saving a Template.

Give it an appropriate name, and then click OK. In the future, when you wish to start from this template, select it from the File menu.

FIGURE 2.5 Opening a File Template

When you are opening a template, notice how there is a choice for "New." This opens your default New File Template. If you wish to alter this file, check "Use as default New Template" while using the Save As Template command. This way, you can use the shortcut Command-n to open up your own, customized template, when creating new projects.

2.6 Multiple Sequences

There will be times when you wish to create a duplicate version or slight variation of your sequence. In this case, it is not necessary to create a new project. It is possible to have more than one sequence in a Digital Performer file.

You can create a new sequence from the Sequence Editor's mini-menu.

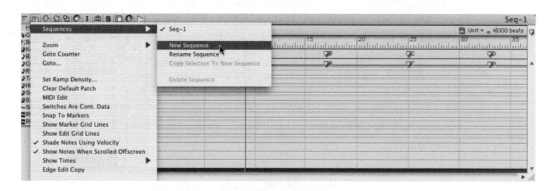

FIGURE 2.6 Creating a New Sequence

You can also give each sequence a name, such as "Upbeat Rock" and "Upbeat Rock Version 2." Once named, it is easy to switch back and forth between the sequences in your file, from the mini-menu.

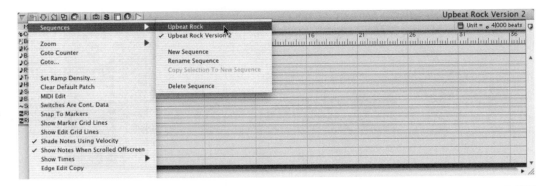

FIGURE 2.7 Switching between Sequences

If you wish to use an exact replica of your sequence as the starting point for your variation, you can do so by selecting all (shortcut: Command-a) and then choosing "Copy Selection To New Sequence."

At this point, we have a grasp of the basic file and hardware structure. Now, let's take a look at the program.

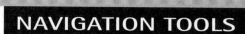

Now that all of your gear is connected, and you've seen some of the basic windows, chapters 3 and 4 will help orient you to Digital Performer's sequencing environment, so that your musical ideas won't be put on hold while you search for buttons.

3.1 The Control Panel

FIGURE 3.1 Control Panel

3.2 Playback Control

The Control Panel looks like a glorified front panel of a CD player. In essence, it functions in a similar manner. It allows you to click Play and Stop, maneuver throughout the sequence, and set a multitude of options. The large buttons in the center function just as one would expect, similar to a CD player or tape deck.

⏮	= Rewind to the beginning of the sequence
⏹	= Stop playback
▶	= Begin playback
⏸	= Pause playback
⏺	= Begin recording
⏮⏭	= Skip forwards or backwards

FIGURE 3.2 Playback Controls

It is important to differentiate between Rewind and Skip Backwards. *Rewind* returns the cursor to the beginning of your sequence. However, it is possible to have more than one sequence in your file. *Skip Backwards* will play-enable the previous sequence.

Keyboard shortcuts are the difference between fast sequencers and slow sequencers, and speed can be the difference between employment and unemployment in the music industry. With that in mind, here are a few keyboard shortcuts to memorize. All, except the spacebar, are on the numeric keypad (laptops must use the Function [fn] key).

SHORTCUT

0	—	Stop
1	—	Rewind
2	—	Pause
3	—	Start recording
ENTER	—	Start
SPACEBAR	—	Toggle playback on and off

3.3 Counters

In the upper right-hand corner of the Control Panel are both the Main Counter and the Auxiliary Counter. These counters indicate the cursor's current location in your sequence, whether you are stopped, paused, playing back, or recording. In figure 3.1, the Main Counter is set to Measures | Beats | Ticks. *Ticks* are a subdivision of the beat. In Digital Performer, there are 480 ticks in a quarter note. Therefore, beat 1, tick 480 is the same as beat 2, tick 000.

These counters can display your location in Measures, Real Time, Time Code, or Samples. To switch the counters, click the small graphic immediately to the right of the counter ▣. In figure 3.1, the Auxiliary Counter is set to "real time."

1|1|000 E = Measures counter

0:00.00 © = Real Time counter

0:00:00:00 ▦ = Time Code counter

0 ♆ = Samples counter

FIGURE 3.3 Counters

The counter settings you will prefer will depend on the kind of project you are working on. If you are composing music, you may prefer to set the Main Counter to "measures" and the Auxiliary Counter to "real time." If you are composing for television and film, you may prefer to set the Main Counter to "measures" and the Auxiliary Counter to "time code." Ultimately, it is your decision how you would like to work.

The decimal key (.) on your number pad will highlight the first section of the main counter, after which you can type the numeric location at which you would like to be located. Pressing the decimal button again will allow you to cycle through the different counter fields. *This is the fastest way to navigate around your sequence.* For instance, if you want to move to measure 102, beat 3, simply type "[decimal]—102—[decimal]—3—[Enter]."

3.4 Tempo Indicator

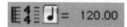

FIGURE 3.4 Tempo Indicator

The *Tempo Indicator* indicates your current tempo setting. It is located directly to the left of the auxiliary counter. When you are using the Tempo Slider as your tempo control, you can highlight the Tempo Indicator and then change it. When you are using the Conductor track as your tempo control, the indicator is solid and cannot be changed. The difference between the Tempo Slider and the Conductor track will be discussed in chapter 5. For now, just think of the Tempo Indicator as a display of your current tempo.

3.5 Metronome, Countoff, and Wait Features

It is often helpful, for beginners and professionals alike, to play/record to a metronome. Digital Performer has a metronome function built into it. The Metronome button is located directly beneath the tempo indicator. Click this button to toggle it on and off. The darkened icon indicates that the metronome is on, and will sound during playback and/or recording.

FIGURE 3.5 Metronome Indicator Button

The metronome has a set of options that designate when it should play and what its source sound should be. If you are not hearing your metronome, check how these options are set. To view these options, double-click the Metronome button.

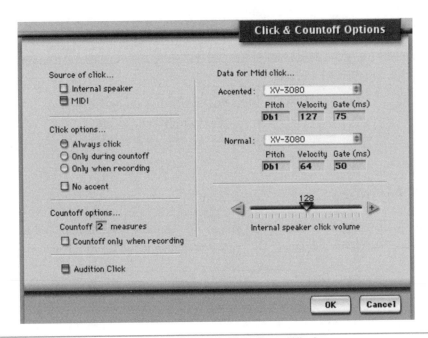

FIGURE 3.6 Metronome Click and Countoff Options Window

In the upper-left corner, MIDI is chosen as the "Source of click. . . ." In this scenario, Digital Performer will generate a MIDI message for each metronome click and send this message to one of your sound modules. The destinations and properties of these messages are determined by the "Data for Midi click..." section on the right. In figure 3.6, I have designated the XV-3080 Channel 10, Db1 (a low-octave D-flat, which is a snare cross-stick sound) to be the instrument that performs the click, which I set louder on the "accented" downbeat (a velocity value of 127, compared to 64) and a longer duration (a gate of 75, compared to 50). You may also set the source of click to your internal speakers. In this case, the click will output through your computer speakers. If you do this, be sure that your sound is not muted in your OSX System Preferences. You can also set the click to play "only when recording," in which case you would not hear it during regular playback. You can also have it play "only during a countoff," as well as adjusting the length and preferences of the countoff.

The Countoff function plays the metronome for a specified duration before beginning playback or recording. If the countoff is activated and set to "2 Bars," the metronome will click eight times (in 4/4 meter) before beginning playback or recording.

The Wait function also counts off before beginning playback, but the length of the countoff is undetermined. Digital Performer is "waiting" for you to send it a MIDI message, such as a "Note On" message or a sustain-pedal message, after which it will begin playback or recording.

Metronome Shortcuts

For speedy users, there are numeric-keypad shortcuts to activate the metronome, the countoff, and the wait function.

NUM LOCK — Turns the metronome on and off.

= — Turns the countoff on and off.

/ — Turns the wait function on and off.

3.6 Memory Cycle

The "Memory Cycle" feature allows you to automatically rewind, stop, and repeat. The boundaries of the Memory Cycle are determined in the Control Panel window.

FIGURE 3.7 Memory Cycle

With this setting, the "Start" boundary is set at the beginning of measure 5, while the "Stop" boundary is set to measure 9. When you click Rewind, the counter jumps back to the Start boundary, rather than the beginning of the sequence. During playback, when the cursor reaches the right boundary, it either stops or returns to the left boundary, depending on what preferences you have set.

In the Control Panel, there are three buttons that are affected by the Memory Cycle settings.

 = Auto Rewind. Normally, when the user clicks Stop, the cursor remains at its current position. When Auto Rewind is activated, clicking Stop returns the cursor to the Start boundary of the Memory Cycle settings.

 = Auto Stop. When Rewind is clicked, the cursor jumps back to the Start boundary of the Memory Cycle setting. However, Digital Performer will also stop playback when it reaches the Stop boundary.

 = Auto Repeat. This causes Digital Performer to loop the defined portion of the sequence, with the Memory Cycle boundaries marking the Start and Stop points of the loop.

Again, keyboard shortcuts are provided on your numeric keypad.

SHORTCUT

7 — Turns Auto Repeat on and off.

8 — Turns Auto Stop on and off.

9 — Turns Auto Rewind on and off.

3.7 Control Panel Drawers

The Control Panel has four side panels (called "drawers") that can be opened by clicking on the small triangle in the upper-right-hand corner of the Control Panel: . Each drawer can be closed by clicking on the small triangle in the upper-right corner of the drawer: ◄. The drawers can be arranged in order by dragging the circle in the lower-right corner of each drawer: ◌.

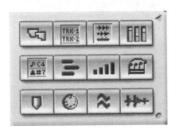

The Windows drawer is a quick way to open various windows.

The Tempo Control drawer lets you assign which tempo device controls playback and other features (see chapter 5).

The Audio drawer lets you set preferences regarding your audio system and audio hardware (see chapter 9).

The Selection drawer displays the boundaries of any selection you make. It also contains a "Memory Play" feature so you can repeatedly play a specific portion of your sequence. It includes "Preroll" and "Postroll" parameters, which add time before and/or after the defined selection boundaries (see chapter 7).

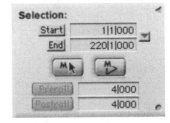

FIGURE 3.7 Control Panel Drawers

These navigation features give you great facility and precise control over how to maneuver around your project. Master the many shortcut keys, and you will find that these tools will bring you much greater efficiency in your work.

SEQUENCE EDITOR

4.1 The Sequence Editor

The Sequence Editor is Digital Performer's primary window for recording, editing, and playing back your project. In previous versions of Digital Performer, many of these tasks were executed in other windows, but as of DP4, it is generally more efficient to use the Sequence Editor, most of the time.

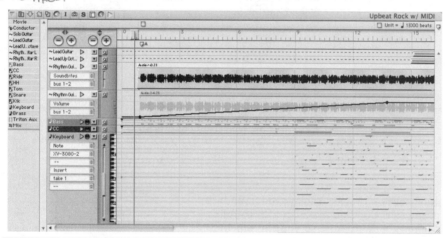

FIGURE 4.1 Sequence Editor

4.2 Title Bar Buttons

The Sequence Editor has several title-bar buttons, which also appear in other Digital Performer windows. These buttons enable the user to control the window's functionality and visibility, as well as the tasks that can be performed there. We'll discuss these title-bar buttons in the context of the Sequence Editor; they have analogous capabilities in other windows.

▽ = **CLOSE BOX.** Closes the Sequence Editor window.

▤ = **MINI–MENU.** Contains multiple commands and preferences specific to each window. In the Sequence Editor, the mini-menu contains zoom settings, sequence settings, alternate editing windows, and more.

= **COLLAPSE**. Collapses the Sequence Editor to OSX's Dock.

= **FALL BEHIND**. Sends the Sequence Editor behind other open windows.

= **RESIZE**. Resizes the Sequence Editor to fit your screen.

= **AUDIBLE MODE**. Turns "Audible Mode" on and off. In the Sequence Editor, Audible Mode will play MIDI when you "scrub" the cursor over it. Likewise, if you click on a single MIDI note, it will sound.

= **INSERT SOUNDBITE**. Lets you add audio to your sequence from the Soundbites window (see section 9.9).

= **AUTOMATIC SNAPSHOT**. Saves a "snapshot" of your automation (see section 11.8).

= **SOLO**. Turns Solo Mode on and off. In Solo Mode, tracks that play are blue, while muted tracks are orange.

= **EXPAND**. Displays a list of your tracks in the upper-left-hand corner of the Sequence Editor. Tracks that you highlight are shown in the Sequence Editor. Tracks that are not highlighted are hidden.

= **AUTOMATIC CONVERSION**. When on, Digital Performer will automatically convert audio files to the appropriate format, sample rate, and bit rate while importing (see section 9.2).

= **AUTO SCROLL**. When on, if the cursor moves beyond the borders of the current screen, the screen will automatically scroll, following to reveal the new region of the sequence.

4.3 Track Types

A *track* is a horizontal representation of data. A track contains all the necessary information about an individual element (such as a MIDI piano part) in a sequence, including the performance itself, inputs, outputs, patch choices, and so on.

The different kinds of tracks are:

CONDUCTOR—Contains sequence-wide information for all instruments, such as tempo, meter, and key changes.

MIDI—Contains MIDI information.

AUDIO—Contains audio information. These tracks can be mono, stereo, or surround sound.

AUXILIARY—Aux tracks are used to route digital audio from one place to another. Think of these as virtual cables. The audio is sent from the Aux track's designated Input to the Aux track's designated Output.

INSTRUMENT—Routes audio from a software sound-source to an audio-hardware driver.

MASTER FADER—Applies volume changes to multiple tracks simultaneously. These volume changes will affect all tracks with the same output as the Master Fader track.

MOVIE—Contains a movie track, showing where each frame of a Quicktime movie falls when imported into Digital Performer.

4.4 Track Information Panel

The Sequence Editor is Digital Performer's most versatile sequencing environment. You can view multiple tracks at different heights and zoom settings, giving you either a broad overview of many tracks or a detailed view of a few tracks. In addition, you can also complete a wide variety of editing tasks. The Sequence Editor can be opened from the Project menu, by typing Shift-s, or from the Windows drawer ▦ .

The Sequence Editor is divided into two primary portions: the Track Information panel and the Track Overview. The Sequence Editor in figure 4.2 displays three tracks: two mono audio tracks and one MIDI track.

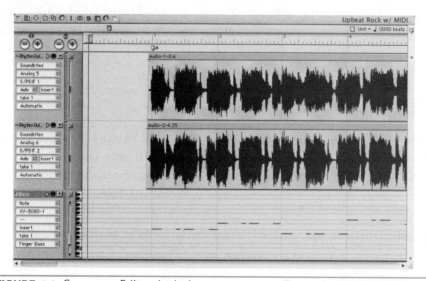

FIGURE 4.2 Sequence Editor. Includes two mono audio tracks and one MIDI track.

To the left of each track is the Track Information panel. Let's look at the Rhythm Guitar audio track's Track Information Panel.

FIGURE 4.3 Track Information Panel

AUDIO TRACK INFORMATION

The top row begins with the Track Type ~ icon, which tells you what kind of track it is. This is a mono audio track, so a single waveform is displayed. For stereo audio tracks, this would be a double waveform ≈, and for MIDI tracks, the icon would be a note ♪. To change the display color of the track, click on the track type icon, and then choose a new color. Using different colors helps you to organize your tracks visually.

Next is the track name Rhythm Gui..., which can be changed by Option-clicking on it. The Play-Enable button ▷ lets you mute or play the track. The Record-Enable button ● lets you determine where newly recorded data will be stored.

The Track Settings menu ▼ contains a variety of preferences for each track. Here, the user is changing the size of the track by making a selection from the Track Settings menu.

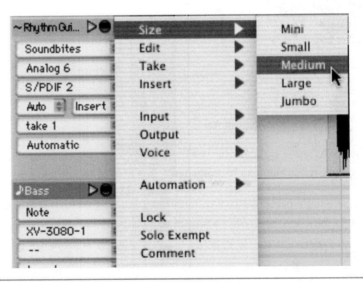

FIGURE 4.4 Track Settings Menu

Next is the Audio Edit row [Soundbites ▾], which determines what type of data will be shown and edited on the track. A *soundbite* is Digital Performer's word for "audio data," so choosing "Soundbites" here lets you see and edit audio. You can also view volume, panning, and other kinds of data.

Below the Audio Edit row is the track's Output [Analog 6 ▾], which determines where the track data is ultimately sent. In this case, "Analog 6" is an output of the audio interface. Most likely, this output is connected to a mixing board, where the Rhythm Guitar part will be connected to a mixer channel.

Below the Output is the track's Input [S/PDIF 1 ▾]. This determines the track's source of input. In this case, the signal coming into the S/PDIF connection of our audio interface will be recorded. Since this is a Rhythm Guitar track, this is most likely an audio signal coming from a guitar preamp, such as a POD or Jstation.

You can also control automation information [Auto ▾] [Insert ▾] from the Sequence Editor (see chapter 11).

The Take feature [take 1 ▾] lets you manage multiple recordings of an instrument part on one track. For instance, if you wish to rerecord the Rhythm Guitar, but do not want to create a new track, you could place multiple takes on one track. Holding on the Take button pops up a menu in which you can add and manage takes.

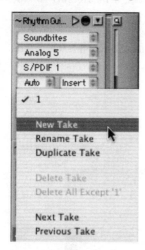

FIGURE 4.5 Take Menu

Below the Take feature is the Audio Voice [Automatic ▾] (see chapter 9). For now, it is best to simply leave this on "Automatic."

If you forget what a particular row or button is (which is nearly inevitable), place your cursor over it and wait. After a second, Digital Performer will display a "hint" label for that feature. Here, Digital Performer is reminding us that the top row is the Audio Edit row.

FIGURE 4.6 Hints. User is given the name of the Audio Edit row.

MIDI TRACK INFORMATION

For MIDI tracks, the Track Information panel is similar, but there are a few differences. The Audio Voice is replaced with a Patch Selection [Fingered Bass], and there is no Automation button. Audio Edit is instead called "MIDI Edit."

FIGURE 4.7 MIDI Track Information Panel. MIDI tracks display the patch selection in the bottom row, here set to "Finger Bass."

4.5 Tracks Overview

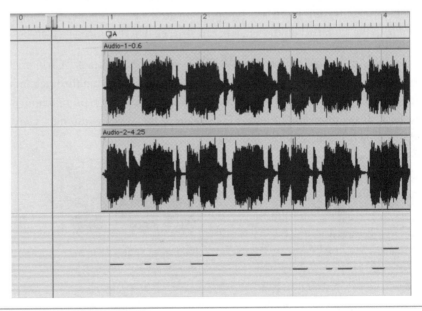

FIGURE 4.8 Tracks Overview

Audio data is represented in the Sequence Editor by waveform diagrams. These are symmetrical diagrams, above and below a horizontal line, showing the amplitude of each sample. A large vertical shape shows a high amplitude sound—a loud noise. Smaller or non-existent waves show softer sounds, or silence. In this way, you can use the waveforms to edit your audio.

MIDI data is represented in the Sequence Editor by horizontal lines, representing the pitch and duration of each MIDI note.

Durations in the Sequence Editor correspond to the Time Ruler, displayed above the tracks. This ruler shows measures subdivided by beats and smaller subdivisions (in this case, sixteenth notes). In this case, the ruler spans from measure 0 to measure 4, beat 2. The two audio tracks begin just before measure 1, while the single MIDI track begins right on measure 1.

It is important to understand how MIDI tracks are structured in the Sequence Editor. Just as the horizontal lines correspond to the time ruler, they also correspond to the piano keyboard icon on the left, which indicates the notes' pitches.

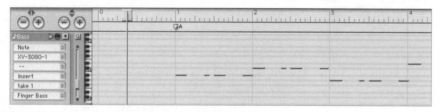

FIGURE 4.9 A MIDI Track

For instance, by looking at the Time Ruler, you can see that the first note on the Bass track begins at measure 1 and lasts for approximately an eighth note. By comparing the note to the keyboard on the left, you can also see that the pitch is a B-flat.

Each track also has a Zoom feature ▣ that is specific to its track. Changing this zoom setting will vertically enlarge or shrink the data's display on the track (not the track size). On audio tracks, this zoom changes only the visual representation of the waveform. It is not raising or lowering the gain of the actual audio file. Here, the audio is shown at a higher magnification.

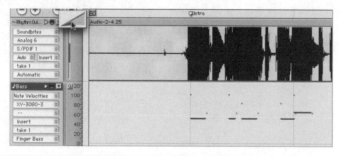

FIGURE 4.10 Audio Viewed at High Magnification

4.6 Manipulating Tracks

The Sequence Editor has many options for customizing your workspace. First, you can zoom in and out both horizontally and vertically using the Zoom buttons in the upper left ⊙⊙ ⊙⊙.

SHORTCUT

COMMAND- → zooms in horizontally.

COMMAND- ← zooms out horizontally.

COMMAND- ↑ zooms in vertically.

COMMAND- ↓ zooms out vertically.

The Sequence Editor also provides customizable zoom settings in its mini-menu. To customize a shortcut, select Zoom–Set Zoom Setting *n*, and it will set the shortcut for Option-Command-*n* to be the current zoom setting. For instance, you could set one zoom setting shortcut to display the entire sequence in your window, another that is zoomed in closely, and another that shows four measures. These zoom settings can then be recalled with easy keyboard shortcuts, such as Option-Command-1. Here, the user is applying the current zoom level of the Time Ruler to setting 1.

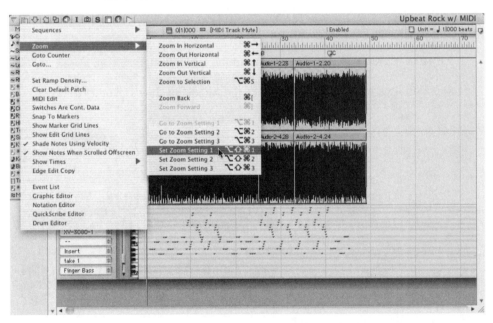

FIGURE 4.11 Sequence Editor. Creating zoom settings from the mini-menu.

Also in the mini-menu, Digital Performer provides Zoom Back (shortcut: Command-[) and Zoom Forward (shortcut: Command-]). These commands let you move forward and backward in a sequence of zoom settings. You can also change your horizontal zoom by Control-dragging on the playback wiper.

You can change the height of an individual track by placing the cursor over the bottom of the Track Information panel. When you do so, the cursor turns into a hand, which you can drag to change the track's height.

FIGURE 4.12 Hand Cursor. Used to change a track's height.

To make all tracks the same height, place the cursor over the bottom of any given track (until the hand appears), and then Option-drag. This applies the new height to all visible tracks.

As mentioned, the Sequence Editor allows you to show or hide any particular tracks. First, highlight the Expand feature ▣ in the title bar. When highlighted, the Track Selector list appears on the left. Highlighted tracks in the list are visible, while those that are not highlighted are hidden.

OPTION–CLICK – Hides all tracks except the one indicated.

SHORTCUT

COMMAND–CLICK – Hides only the track indicated, but shows all other tracks.

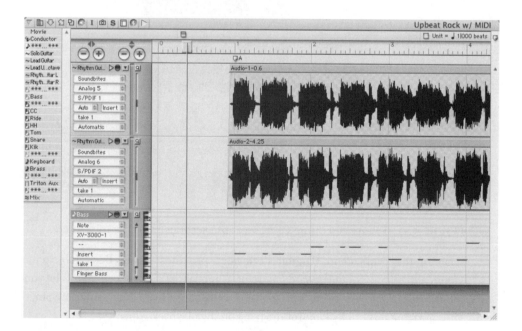

FIGURE 4.13 Expand Feature On

In this window (figure 4.13), the two Rhythm Guitars and Bass are shown, while everything else is hidden.

In addition, you can reorder tracks up and down. To do so, place the cursor over the left edge of the Tracks Information Panel. When you do so, the cursor will change, and you can then drag the track to its new destination.

FIGURE 4.14 Move Cursor. Used to rearrange track order.

In figure 4.15, the Bass track has been moved above the Rhythm Guitar tracks.

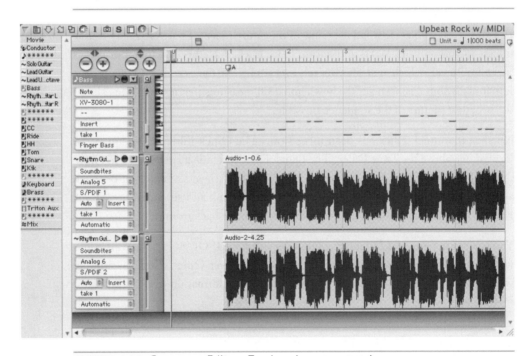

FIGURE 4.15 Sequence Editor. Track order rearranged.

4.7 Sequence Editor Example Layouts

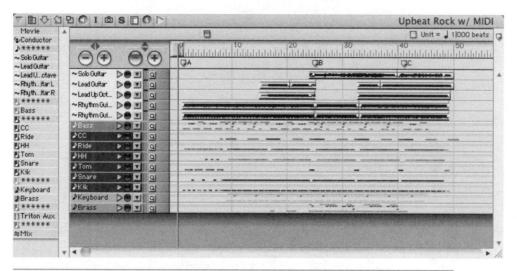

FIGURE 4.16 Sequence Editor. Example 1.

In figure 4.16, you get a broad overview of the entire piece. There are many visible tracks, including both MIDI and audio. The tracks have been reduced in height to "mini" level, which will let you see everything on the screen. Likewise, the horizontal zoom has been set to show almost 60 measures per screen. This shows the broadest picture of the sequence possible.

Notably, the Quick Filter has been turned on. The Quick Filter is the square located just above the Time Ruler. The Quick Filter will hide all of the data not from the top layer of each track. Every track can have multiple layers of information, such as MIDI Notes, Velocities, Volume, Panning, Pitch Bend, and so on. When Quick Filter is off, all of these other layers will be shown in the background.

You can see in figure 4.17 that the result is very cluttered. Of course, there are times when you will want to see this extra information. However, Quick Filter can simplify what you are looking at, displaying just the amount of information you have to digest immediately.

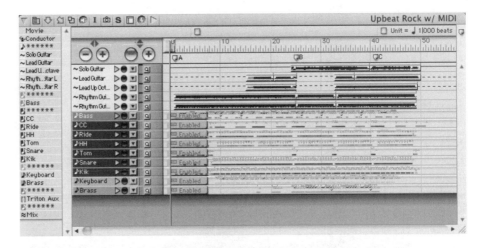

FIGURE 4.17 Quick Filter Off. Notice how cluttered the screen is.

The setup in figure 4.18 is very useful. All the tracks in the piece are visible, with all but the Bass track minimized. This allows you to see what is going on in all tracks, while getting a detailed veiw of the Bass part.

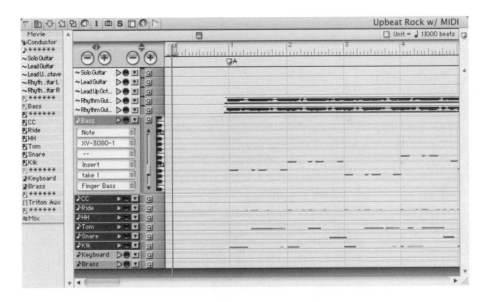

FIGURE 4.18 Quick Filter On. Only MIDI notes and audio soundbites are visible.

In figure 4.19, only the Keyboard part is shown, and it is enlarged both vertically and horizontally. While this does not give us information regarding the other tracks, we can edit the Keyboard part in very fine detail.

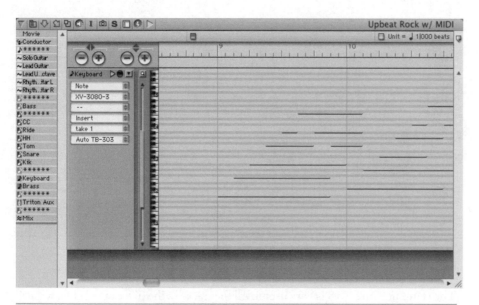

FIGURE 4.19 Keyboard Part. Setup for detailed editing.

FILE SETUP

So far, we have discussed a lot of technical issues to get you up, running, and familiar with your environment. Now, let's talk about some music.

In this chapter, we will discuss one particular piece of music, "Upbeat Rock," and the best way to set up your file for it.

Begin by creating a new project file (File–New). Call it "Upbeat Rock." Switch to the Sequence Editor window, and notice that by default, new files come with the Conductor track, four MIDI tracks, and four audio tracks.

5.1 "Upbeat Rock" Example

Figure 5.1 shows the score of "Upbeat Rock," which we will create in Digital Performer over the next few chapters.

TRACK 1

FIGURE 5.1 Upbeat Rock

FIGURE 5.1 Upbeat Rock (continued)

FIGURE 5.1 Upbeat Rock (continued)

FIGURE 5.1 Upbeat Rock (continued)

FIGURE 5.1 Upbeat Rock (continued)

FIGURE 5.1 Upbeat Rock (continued)

5.2 Create Appropriate Tracks

For this project, we must record drums, bass, keyboard, brass, and guitar parts. We'll start by recording the drums, bass, keyboard, and brass on MIDI tracks. We will record the guitar to audio tracks, later on.

It is always best to place each instrument in its own individual track. This will maximize your ability to edit and mix your music. For instance, it would be possible to record the drums all to a single MIDI track. However, if you place the snare on its own track, the bass drum on its own track, and so on, you will be able to edit and control them independently, and ultimately, have better control over how the whole drum set sounds. With this in mind, we should create six drum tracks (crash cymbals, ride cymbal, hi-hats, toms, snare drum, and bass drum). We will also need MIDI tracks for the bass, keyboard, and brass, totaling nine MIDI tracks for this project.

To create these MIDI tracks, choose Project–Add Tracks–MIDI Track (shortcut: Shift-Command-m).

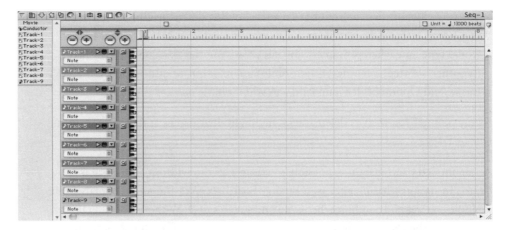

FIGURE 5.2 MIDI Tracks Created

Add three mono audio tracks for the guitar: two for rhythm guitars and one for a lead guitar. To add the audio tracks, choose Project–Add Track–Mono Audio Track (shortcut: Shift-Command-a).

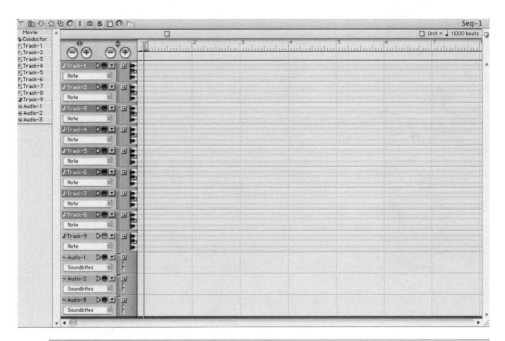

FIGURE 5.3 MIDI and Audio Tracks Created

Figure 5.3 shows the Sequence Editor for the new file, soon to become rock high art. It currently contains nine MIDI tracks and three audio tracks. In addition, every Digital Performer file contains a Conductor track and Movie track, neither of which can be deleted.

You can add more than one track at a time by holding down the Option key while you select Add Track. In this case, you would need nine MIDI tracks, so you would type nine when prompted, and click OK. You can also combine this with the other shortcuts, typing Option-Shift-Command-m to add multiple MIDI tracks, and Option-Shift-Command-a to add multiple mono audio tracks.

SHORTCUT

At any point, if you wish to delete tracks, highlight their names and choose Project–Delete Tracks.

As mentioned previously, it is possible to create a studio without a physical mixing board. In its most basic capacity, a mixing board receives the audio signals from multiple sources and combines them into one stereo signal. Without a mixing board, this task can be also accomplished with a series of Aux tracks. One Aux track will be required for each sound module. Since we will be using two sound modules, two Aux tracks are necessary. To add an Aux track, choose Project–Add Track–Aux Track (shortcut: Control-Command-a).

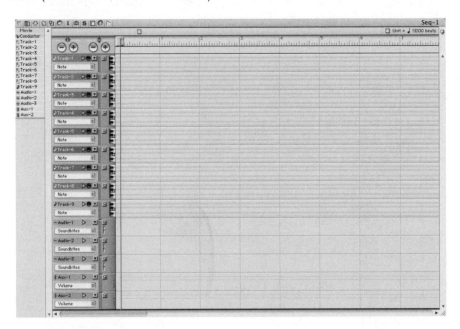

FIGURE 5.4 MIDI, Audio and Aux Tracks Created

You can add more than one Aux track at a time by holding down the Option and Shift key while you select Add Track.

SHORTCUT

If you have a mixing board in your studio, you do not need to create these Aux tracks.

In addition, we will create one instrument track. An instrument track will allow us to utilize one software sound source. A *software sound source* is a sampler or synthesizer packaged as a software program, rather than a hardware device.

FIGURE 5.5 Creating a New Instrument Track

*OSX has created a standard format for audio plug-ins called "Audio Units." Audio Units appear at Project–Add Track–Instrument Track. When you create an instrument track, the interface of your software sound source will appear, allowing you to select and edit sounds.

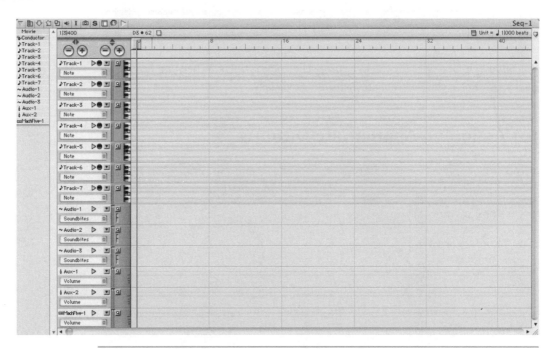

FIGURE 5.6 MIDI, Audio, Aux, and Instrument Tracks Created

Now we have all of the tracks we will need for "Upbeat Rock."

5.3 Name Tracks

It is important to name each track. To name tracks, Option-click on the Track Name field. These names will help you to visually organize your file. In addition, the track names will help you differentiate information when using other windows, as well as playing a role in determining the names of audio files, when you record.

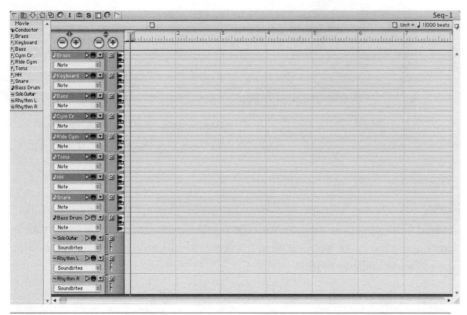

FIGURE 5.7 Tracks Named

It is often helpful to give the tracks appropriate color settings. When you have many tracks, this helps you differentiate instruments visually.

5.4 Assigning Appropriate Outputs

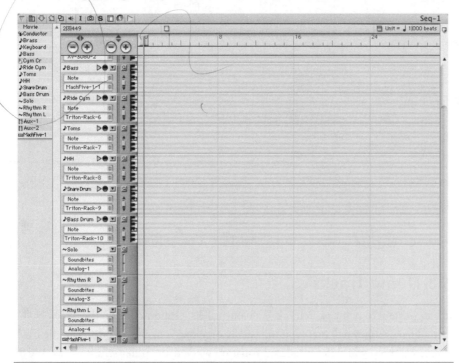

FIGURE 5.8 Track Outputs Assigned

In order to hear the instrument on each track, we need to properly route the track's *output*. This refers to the destination of the track's data when Digital Performer is playing back the sequence.

STUDIOS WITH MIXING BOARDS

It works differently for audio and MIDI tracks. Audio track outputs refer to the outputs of your audio interface. In figure 5.6, the audio tracks are routed to Analog 1, 3, and 4. Consequently, the information on these tracks will leave outputs Analog 1, 3, and 4 of the audio interface, which should be connected to a mixing board. The mixing board will output to an amplifier and speakers.

MIDI track outputs refer to your MIDI sound sources—most commonly, your sound modules. Once the MIDI data is sent to the sound module, it is then converted into audio. Sound modules have audio out ports, which must be connected to your mixing board, amplifier, and speakers.

The output name of a MIDI track has two parts: the name of the sound module and the sound module's "channel" number. For instance, the brass track is assigned to XV-3080-1. This means all the MIDI information on this track will be sent to the sound module called XV-3080, which was declared in Audio MIDI Setup. The XV-3080 will in turn play this track's output on its channel 1.

A "channel" is a path for MIDI data. When most MIDI messages travel over a MIDI cable, they travel on a particular channel, numbered 1 to 16. This means a MIDI cable can transmit information about sixteen different performances at one time. Consequently, most sound modules can receive and send MIDI messages on up to sixteen channels. When you are setting MIDI outputs, you must choose between channel 1 and 16 on each given sound module.

SHORTCUT ▶ Digital Performer provides keyboard shortcuts that allow you to quickly change outputs of MIDI tracks. First, highlight the track name. Next, Shift-↑ and Shift-↓ will cycle you through your available MIDI devices. Option-↑ and Option-↓ cycle you through the available channels on the current device.

In figure 5.8, notice that each MIDI track has a unique output. Many parameters, such as patch, volume, and panning, can have only one setting per channel. Just as you cannot watch two shows simultaneously on one television channel, you cannot play two parts simultaneously on one channel of your sound module. For this reason, the keyboard and bass must be on separate channels, and so on.

Traditionally, channel 10 is used exclusively for drum and percussion sounds. In fact, many sound modules will limit you to choosing drum sounds only on channel 10. If this is the case, it will limit your drum track outputs to channel 10 of your given sound module. If you are not limited by this, it is best to place your drum elements on individual outputs to increase editing and mixing flexibility.

Studios without Mixing Boards

If you are not using a mixing board, connect the audio outputs of your sound modules to the audio inputs of your audio interface. For our example, we will connect the XV-3080 to analog inputs 3–4 and the Triton-Rack to analog inputs 5–6. This will allow us to manipulate their audio signals from within Digital Performer.

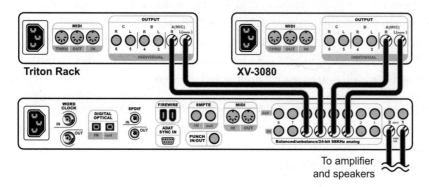

FIGURE 5.9   Sound Modules Connected to the Audio Interface

Your audio interface will not automatically route the audio coming in its inputs to its main outputs. This is why you created Aux tracks. Think of an Aux track as a virtual cable. It routes audio from one place (the input of the Aux track) to another (the output of the Aux track).

In figure 5.10, the track titled "Aux-1" is set to route audio from Input Analog 3–4 to Output Analog 1–2. In our example, this effectively routes the audio from the XV-3080 to the amplifier/speakers.

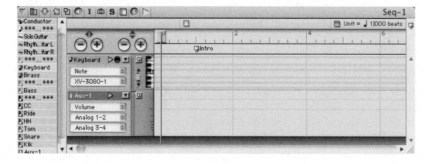

FIGURE 5.10   XV-3080 Aux Track Inputs and Outputs Assigned

In figure 5.11, the track titled "Aux-2" is set to route audio from Input Analog 5–6 to output Analog 1–2. In our example, this effectively routes the audio from the Triton Rack to the amplifier/speakers.

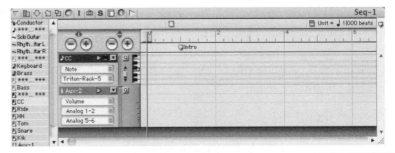

FIGURE 5.11 Triton Aux Track Inputs and Outputs Assigned

The function of an instrument track is similar to that of an Aux track. It is also a "virtual cable" that routes audio from one place to another. In the case of an instrument track, the audio travels from the name of the track—your software sound source—to the output of the track—an output on your audio interface. As mentioned in section 1.12, Digital Performer can interact with three types of virtual instruments: AU, MAS, and Rewire. An instrument track is utilized when setting up an AU or MAS instrument.

In figure 5.12, the audio signal will travel from MachFive, MOTU's software sampler, to outputs Analog 1–2.

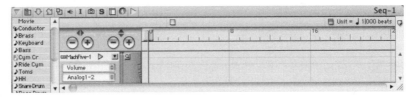

FIGURE 5.12 Instrument Track. Output Assigned

Working in tandem with your instrument track, you will need at least one MIDI track. This track will send MIDI information to your sound source, which will create the corresponding audio and route this to the output determined by the instrument track. In figure 5.13, the Bass track is outputting MIDI to MachFive. In turn, MachFive is outputting the corresponding audio to Analog 1–2.

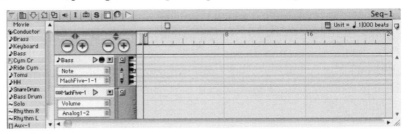

FIGURE 5.13 MIDI Track Output Assigned for Software Sound Source.

Notice that the combined effect of these outputs allows us to proceed without a mixing board. Remember, the fundamental function of a mixing board is to combine the signals from several sources into one stereo signal. In figure 5.14, the audio from the sound modules, software sound source, and audio tracks are all being sent to Analog 1–2, producing a single stereo mix. The other roles of a mixing board, such as setting levels and assigning effects, can be performed with Digital Performer's internal mixing board (see chapter 11).

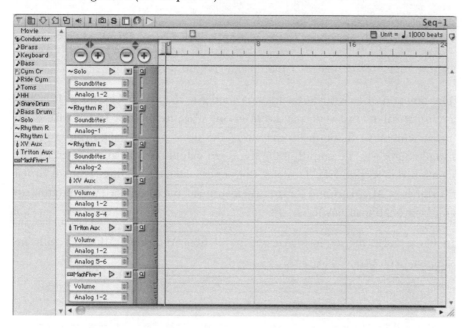

FIGURE 5.14 Inputs and Outputs for Aux, Audio, and Instrument Tracks

Unlike AU and MAS instruments, Rewire does not use an instrument track. Reason is a software program that utilizes Rewire to communicate with other programs. When Reason is launched in Rewire mode, it is capable of communicating with other sequencers, including Digital Performer. To open Reason in Rewire mode, first open Digital Performer, then open Reason. Reason will detect Digital Performer, automatically opening in Rewire mode.

Again, you will need two tracks in Digital Performer: one to send MIDI to Reason, and another to properly route the audio. In figure 5.15, there is one MIDI track whose output is Reason. Reason then converts this MIDI into the appropriate audio, sending it out the Mix outputs. In Digital Performer, an Aux track routes the audio from Reason's Mix output to Analog 1–2 of our audio hardware, presumably then sending it to speakers, headphones, or a mixing board.

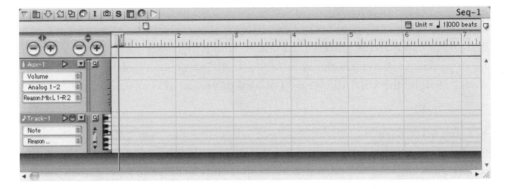

FIGURE 5.15 Reason Tracks

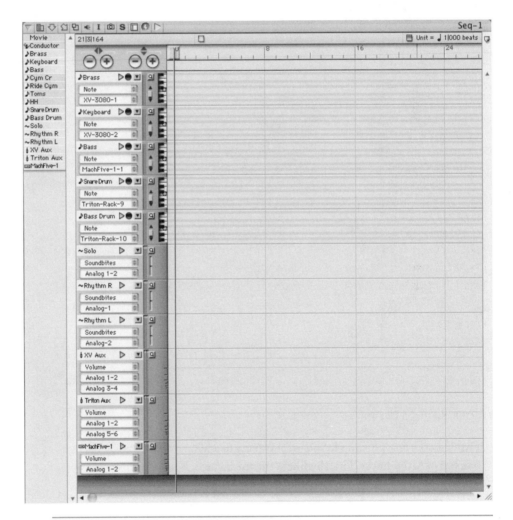

FIGURE 5.16 All Outputs Assigned

Now we have all of the Outputs assigned that we will need for "Upbeat Rock."

5.5 Assign Patches

Next, select appropriate *patches* (instrument sounds) for each MIDI track. The Patch parameter is at the bottom row of the Track Information panel. To select a sound, click on the MIDI Patch row. This will display all of your sound module's banks and patches.

In figure 5.17, "New R&R Brass" has been selected for the brass, "Auto TB-303" has been selected for the keyboard, and so on. These selections are *default* patch settings, meaning they will take affect every time you click Play at the beginning of the sequence.

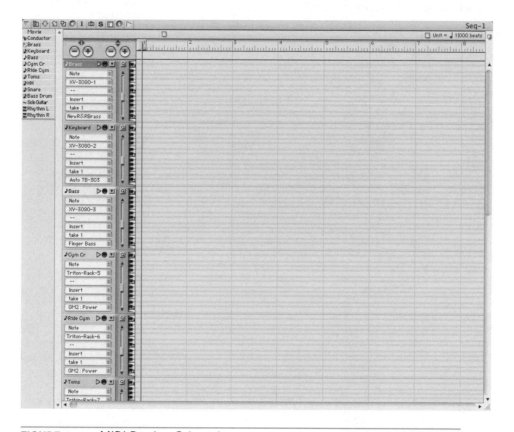

FIGURE 5.17 MIDI Patches Selected.

Digital Performer provides keyboard shortcuts that allow you to quickly change patches of MIDI tracks. First, highlight the track name. Next, Ctrl-↑ and Ctrl-↓ will cycle you through your available patches.

BEWARE: Most sound modules have more than one playback mode. One particular mode is intended for use with an external sequencer, while the other modes can only play back one sound at a time. The names of the modes will vary from brand to brand, and you will need to get to know your sound module. For sequencing purposes, most Rolands require "Perform" mode and most Korgs require "Seq" mode.

How do you select patches for your software sound sources? This will depend entirely upon your sound source. The patch typically will not be selected in Digital Performer's MIDI track, but rather the interface of the software sound source.

Once you set your patches, your band is set up.

5.6 Set Tempo

CONDUCTOR TRACK VERSUS TEMPO SLIDER

Digital Performer has two internal clocks that can dictate the tempo. The first is the Conductor track. When using the Conductor track, you can create a detailed map of the tempo throughout the song. Your tempo can speed up and slow down many times. Any information in the Conductor track will appear in the top track of the Sequence Editor, labeled "Conductor."

The second internal clock is called the "Tempo Slider." You cannot create detailed tempo changes in the Tempo Slider. However, it is useful when wanting to quickly change the tempo to check the "feel" of a piece in another tempo or to slow the tempo down to play in difficult parts.

How do you know which one Digital Performer is following? The Control Panel has a Tempo drawer that determines whether Digital Performer is following the tempo slider or the Conductor track. In the following graphic, the Conductor track is selected.

FIGURE 5.18 Control Panel and Tempo Drawer. Here, the Conductor track is the selected tempo control.

CHANGING THE CONDUCTOR TRACK

To easily change the tempo in the Conductor track, select Project Menu–Modify Conductor Track–Change Tempo.

FIGURE 5.19 Changing Tempo from the Project Menu

After selecting "Change Tempo," the Change Tempo window will appear.

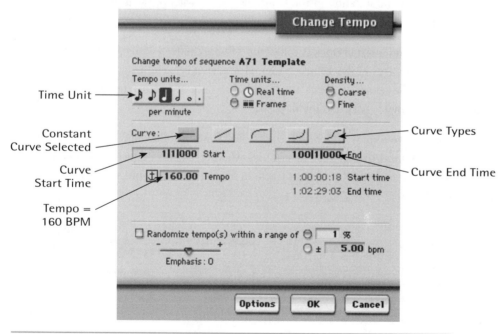

FIGURE 5.20 Change Tempo Window

To set an initial tempo, you must assign a time unit and a tempo. In figure 5.20, a quarter note is set to equal 160 BPM. This matches the metronome marking of "Upbeat Rock."

When you are setting tempo with this window, you are created a tempo curve. You must set the curve type, start point, and end point. If you are setting the tempo at the beginning of your sequence, you will set the start point to the beginning of your sequence, and mostly likely select a constant curve ▬. With the settings in figure 5.20, the tempo will be set to 160 BPM at measure 1 and remain so for the entire sequence.

When setting the tempo, the End Time *must* be greater than the Start Time. If you set both to 1|1|000, you will not be able to click "OK."

To create an accelerando or ritard, select a different curve type, such as linear ◢. Here, you must set a start and end point, as well as a start and end tempo. In figure 5.21, an accelerando will be created in measure 4 that speeds up the tempo from 80 to 160 BPM.

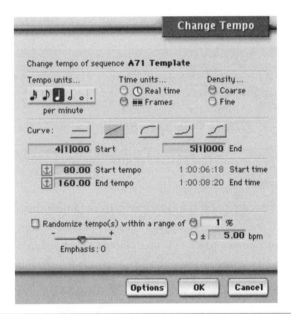

FIGURE 5.21   Creating an Accelerando.

The tempo in the Conductor track can also be changed from the Sequence Editor. As with MIDI and Audio tracks, the Conductor track contains an information panel.

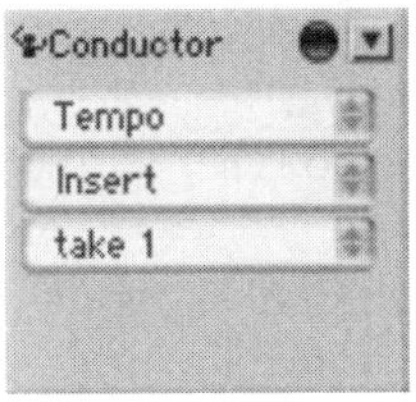

FIGURE 5.22   Track Information Panel for the Conductor Track

To create a tempo change, choose Insert–Tempo Change.

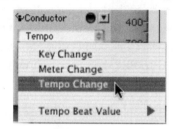

FIGURE 5.23 Conductor Track. Inserting a tempo change.

At this point, the cursor will turn into a Pencil, and you can insert the new tempo in the Conductor track. As with MIDI and audio data, a tempo change will correspond to the Time Ruler. The Conductor track has a scale from 0 to 400 on the left.

Pointer Coordinates

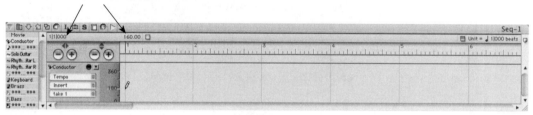

FIGURE 5.24 Conductor Track. Pencil inserting a tempo change of 160 BPM at measure 1.

As you move the Pencil around the Conductor track, notice that its exact location is displayed in the pointer coordinate indicators. When inserting a tempo change at the beginning of your sequence, it is acceptable to click before the first measure. This will result in the tempo change being placed exactly at the beginning of your sequence.

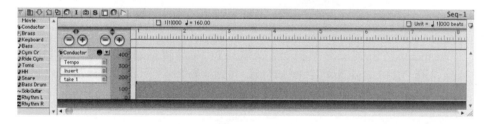

FIGURE 5.25 Conductor Track. Tempo is set to 160 BPM.

In figure 5.25, a tempo change has been added at measure 1, beat 1, tick 000, changing the tempo to 160 BPM. Notice how this information is detailed just to the right of the Quick Filter ⬚ 1|1|000 ♩ = 160.00 . This is because a newly inserted tempo change is automatically selected. Any time a single event is selected in the Sequence Editor, its specific properties are detailed in this area.

Once the Conductor Edit row is set to Tempo, you can create very detailed tempo changes by drawing them with the Pencil. To change the cursor to a Pencil, type the letter *P* on your keyboard twice. Then draw to your heart's delight. Notice that the shape of what you draw will be determined by the "Reshape Flavor" in the Tools Palette.

In figure 5.26, an accelerando has been created that speeds up the tempo from 80 BPM to 160 BPM during measures 4 and 5.

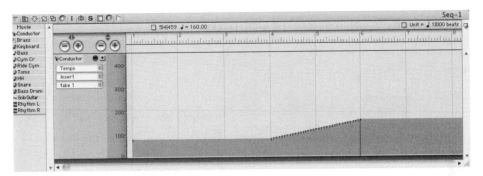

FIGURE 5.26 Conductor Track. Accelerando created.

CHANGING THE TEMPO SLIDER

To set the Tempo Slider, in the Tempo drawer, switch from the Conductor track to the Tempo Slider. Then, drag the blue triangle left and right. As you do so, watch the tempo in the tempo indicator change. In this case, the Tempo Slider is set to 132.00. When the Tempo Slider is activated, you can also just type a number in the Tempo Indicator field.

FIGURE 5.27 Control Panel and Tempo Drawer. Switched to Tempo Slider.

CONDUCTOR TRACK VERSUS TEMPO SLIDER CONCLUSION

Given both tools, what is the best way to use the Tempo Slider and the Conductor track? Ultimately, it is up to each user to decide how they wish to work. However, the setup outlined above is a good way to start. Think of the Conductor track as the performance tempo, and the Tempo Slider as a convenient way to set a temporary tempo during the production process.

So, set the Conductor track to the intended performance tempo(s) of the piece. This allows you to add tempo changes if the need arises. Second, set the Tempo Slider to a somewhat slower tempo. This way, if you run into a part that is difficult to perform, you can quickly switch to the Tempo Slider. At the slower tempo, you can record an impeccable performance, and then switch back to the Conductor track to listen to it at the desired performance tempo. You will sound like Beethoven. In the case of our "Upbeat Rock" tune, the actual tempo is 160 BPM, so a logical tempo for the tempo slider might be 132 BPM.

ADDITIONAL CONDUCTOR TRACK DATA

You can also make meter and key changes in the Conductor track. Both features are accessible via the Project Menu.

FIGURE 5.28 Change Meter

Key Changes will not affect the pitches in any way. Rather, the key change will determine how the data appears in the Notation Editors and how note names are spelled in the Event List and other data display areas. These editors can be used to edit MIDI and print out scores/parts (see chapter 8).

Notably, it is also possible to create meter and key changes with the Sequence Editor's Insert feature. If you choose this route, be sure you are not creating partial measures with your Meter changes. If partial measures become a problem for you, they can avoided entirely by activating "Fix partial measures automatically" in your preferences (Digital Performer Menu–Preferences).

After setting the tempo, meter, and key in "Upbeat Rock," our Sequence Editor window looks like figure 5.29.

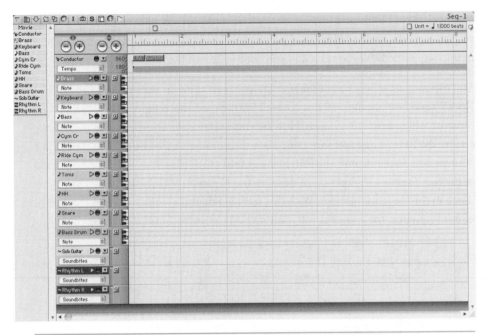

FIGURE 5.29 "Upbeat Rock" with Conductor Track Settings

5.7 Change the Start Time of Your Sequence

Avoid having music starting at the very beginning of your sequence, as doing so will likely lead to timing errors in your playback. Think of the amount of information at measure 1, beat 1, tick 000. Each track is sending a patch change, volume setting, panning settings, and so on. If you also have Note On messages at 1/1/000, they will not trigger in time.

To avoid this, always start your music in the second measure of the sequence.

Of course, this means the music will start at what the Sequence Editor indicates, by default, as measure 2. You can avoid this by having the first measure of the Sequence Editor be measure 0. Set this preference in the Tempo Control drawer. Click on the "Start Times…" button.

FIGURE 5.30 Start Times

You will then be given a dialog box where you can set the beginning of your sequence. Here, set the "Measures" parameter to zero. This will set the first measure in the Sequence Editor to zero, and so your music will begin at measure 1.

You can also set where your sequence starts in real time. In the case of our "Upbeat Rock" tune, we should set this to –0:01.50. Since the tempo is 160 BPM, one measure will pass in 1.5 seconds. How do you find this duration at any tempo? After setting the Start Time measure to 0, place the cursor at measure 1. The Real Time counter will display a time, 0:01.50 in the case of 160 BPM. This is the time duration of the first measure. Simply make this number negative, and set the Real Time Start Time to this negative number. With this setting, when we reach the second measure of our sequence, the counters will indicate both measure 1 and second 0.

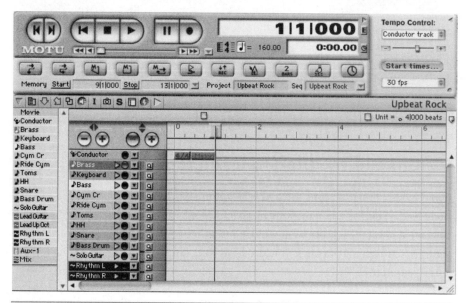

FIGURE 5.31 "Upbeat Rock" with Start Times Set

5.8 Markers

Markers are text labels for our sequence, and they can be a helpful way to organize our projects. They serve the same function as rehearsal letters, helping us to easily navigate to various points of our sequence. We might put a marker at every verse, chorus, bridge, coda, or wherever else they can be helpful. They have no effect on playback.

Once all the instruments, tempos, and meter markings are set, our file looks great. It is a good time to add markers to outline the form of the music. One easy way to create a marker is to drag from the marker in the upper-right-hand corner of the Sequence Editor ▣, dropping the marker just below the Time Ruler. In this manner, we can create markers outlining the major sections of "Upbeat Rock."

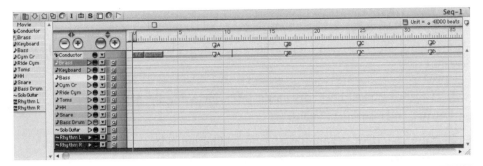

FIGURE 5.32 Upbeat Rock. Sections outlined with Markers.

You can quickly create a marker by typing Control-m, which creates a marker at the location of your cursor. To rename a marker, double-click it in the Conductor track.

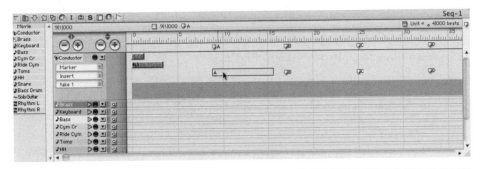

FIGURE 5.33 Editing Markers in the Conductor Track

In the Conductor track, you can move markers by dragging them, or delete them by highlighting them and hitting Delete.

Clicking on the marker just below the Time Ruler highlights your entire sequence from that point until the next marker. For example, in the file above, if we clicked on Marker A on the ruler, everything between Markers A and B would be highlighted: measures 9 through 17. This can be particularly handy when copying and pasting large sections. For instance, if you are writing a pop tune, you may wish to copy the instrumental background of verse 1 and paste it at verses 2 and 3. If your markers are set up properly, this would be very easy to do.

5.9 Review

At this point, our file is ready for us to start recording. The steps we took to get here were:

1. Create the tracks necessary for the piece, including any MIDI, audio, Aux, and instrument tracks.

2. Give each track an appropriate name by Option-clicking on each track name.

3. Assign appropriate outputs. Be sure each individual MIDI instrument has a unique output.

4. For Aux tracks, assign appropriate inputs.

5. Select patches.

6. Set the tempo of the piece in the Conductor track.

7. Set a slower tempo in the Tempo Slider.

8. Set the time and key signature in the Conductor track.

9. Set the Start Time to Measure 0 and an appropriate Real Time.

10. Place appropriate markers to outline the structure of the piece.

RECORDING MIDI

6.1 Record Enable

To record a performance, whether it is MIDI or audio, you must indicate to Digital Performer which track should record the data. This is done by record-enabling the target track(s). A Record-Enable button 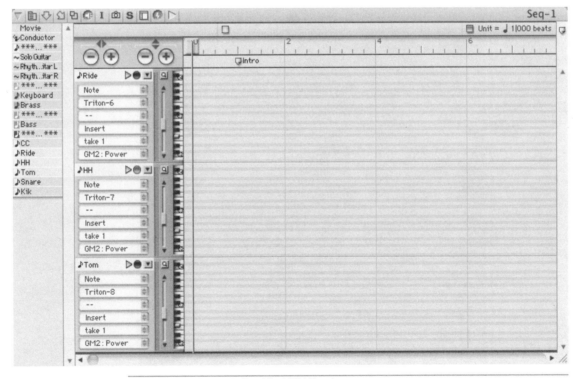 is located on each track, present in the Sequence Editor, Tracks window, and Mixing Board. This button determines which track(s) will receive the data you are recording. This is a simple but important concept. In the following graphic, the HH (hi-hat) track is record-enabled. This means that when you record, whatever you play on your MIDI keyboard will be placed onto the HH track.

FIGURE 6.1 Record-Enabled HH Track

In addition, since the HH track's output is Triton-Rack-7, this information will be sent to the Triton-Rack sound module. The Triton will play it back on its eighth channel—subject to the patch and volume settings of channel 7. We have assigned this channel to a drum kit, which traditionally produces hi-hat sounds on F#1, G#1, and A#1.

UP ARROW (↑) sends the record-enable button up one track.

DOWN ARROW (↓) sends the record-enable button down one track.

6.2 Recording MIDI

To record MIDI, record-enable your target track, click Record, and perform the part. Then record-enable the next part and repeat. Remember, if a particular MIDI part is too difficult, you can switch to the Tempo Slider, which you can set to a slower tempo (see chapter 5).

BASS DRUM

For the most part, you must record elements one at a time. The order in which you do so, ultimately, is up to you. With "Upbeat Rock," we will begin with the bass drum part.

In the following example, the Bass Drum part of "Upbeat Rock" has been recorded.

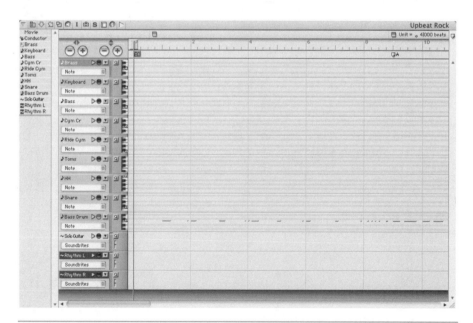

FIGURE 6.2 Bass Drum Track with Recorded MIDI

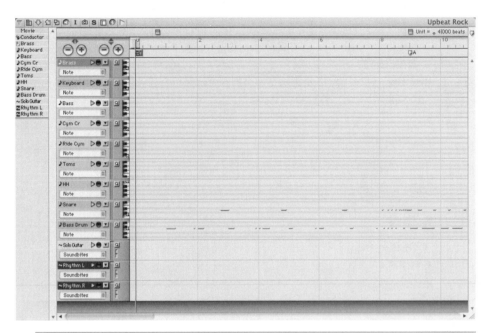

FIGURE 6.3 Bass and Snare Drum Track with Recorded MIDI

SNARE DRUM

Next, change the record-enable button to the Snare part, rewind, and record the snare.

REMAINING DRUMS

In the same manner, we progress through the drums, recording each part as we go. If you feel comfortable recording more than one element at a time, by all means feel free to do so. For instance, it is often preferable to record the bass and snare drum simultaneously. If you do so, separate them into individual tracks after recording so that you will have the most mixing flexibility. Moving recorded data around will be covered in chapter 7.

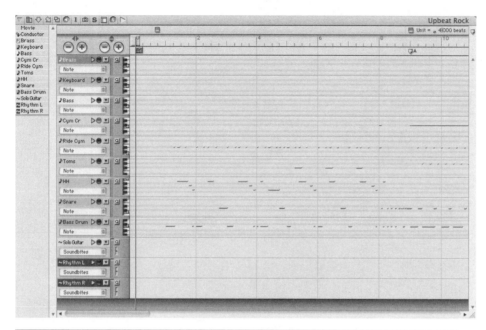

FIGURE 6.4 All Drum Tracks with Recorded MIDI

BASS, KEYBOARD, AND BRASS

Recording instrumentals will be no different from recording drums. Simply rewind, record-enable, and record.

FIGURE 6.5 Bass, Keyboard, and Brass Tracks Recorded with MIDI

6.3 Additional Recording Techniques

OVERDUB

FIGURE 6.6 Overdub Button in the Control Panel

Typically, Digital Performer erases the previous contents of a MIDI track while you record. However, there are times in which you will wish to keep this material, while recording an additional element on top. To do so, activate the Overdub feature in the Control Panel.

PUNCH-IN

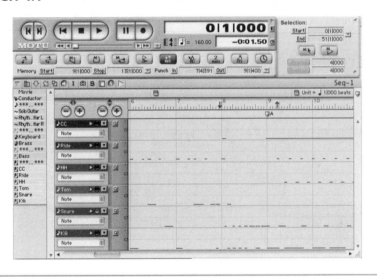

FIGURE 6.7 Punch-In Activated in the Control Panel

Punch-In recording allows you to record during a specific time period in the track. In figure 6.7, Punch-In is set to begin recording just before measure 8 and stop just after measure 9. Since the Snare track is record-enabled, this will record over the snare fill in measure 8.

When Punch-In is activated, the punch-in data appears in the bottom-right of the Control Panel ⟨Punch In 7|4|391 Out 9|1|400⟩. This data is also represented by the red arrows in the Sequence Editor's time ruler ⟨↓........↑⟩. The In and Out points can be changed in several ways. You can drag the red arrows left and right. You also can click directly in the numeric fields ⟨7|4|391⟩ in the Control Panel, type a change, and hit Enter. Clicking directly on the "In" ⟨In 7|4|391⟩ and "Out" ⟨Out 9|1|400⟩ buttons sets the coordinates to the current location of the cursor. In addition, there is a menu to the right of the numeric fields that provides useful options.

FIGURE 6.8 Punch-In Menu

6.4 What If I Don't Play Keyboards?

Since the most common MIDI controller is the keyboard, musicians who do not play piano often feel left out of the loop. If this is you, you essentially have three options: using Step Record, using the Pencil tool, or using your keyboard at a reduced tempo.

STEP RECORD

FIGURE 6.9 Step-Record Window

The Step-Record window can be opened from the Studio menu (shortcut: Command-8). This allows you to record a performance at whatever pace you need. First, select the duration of the note you wish to enter. Then play the note or chord on your keyboard. The note will be created on the track selected in the "Recording On" field, and placed at the location indicated in "Current Step." Use the Motion Buttons on the right to navigate the sequence.

DRAWING NOTES

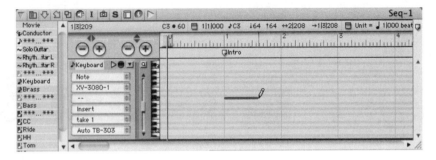

FIGURE 6.10 Inserting Notes with the Pencil

You also can insert notes with the Pencil tool from the Tools Palette. The note will be created where you click. The duration can be determined by dragging. Both of these elements will be controlled by the "Edit Resolution" button, when it is activated. As usual, holding the Command key will toggle the "Edit Resolution" button on and off.

USING YOUR KEYBOARD

While these techniques are useful, they can produce rather rigid performances. Your results will be the most musical if you perform on your keyboard. If necessary, you can slow the tempo down with the tempo slider. Don't forget, you can use the Overdub feature to add elements on a second pass. Also, your performance doesn't need to be perfect. We will discuss many ways to edit and refine your performance in chapter 7.

EDITING YOUR MIDI PERFORMANCE

Digital Performer gives you complete control of your performance, allowing you to edit every aspect of your MIDI data. While the original performance is important, proper editing can heal many performance wounds, and it gives you a refined, polished final product.

7.1 Tools Palette

The Tools palette can be opened by choosing Studio–Tools or with the Shift-o shortcut. Each tool in the palette allows you to perform a different task, and it will be discussed frequently regarding editing both MIDI and audio.

FIGURE 7.1 Editing Tools Palette

Each tool can be accessed three ways.

1. Open the Tools palette, and select the desired tool with the cursor.

2. Use each tool's assigned shortcut key. If you hold down the key on your ASCII keyboard, the cursor will temporarily turn into the desired tool. It will turn back when you lift the key.

3. If you double-tap the keyboard shortcut key, the cursor permanently changes to the desired tool.

= **MARQUEE TOOL**, sometimes called the "pointer." Primarily used to select and move data objects, such as notes, though its exact functionality varies greatly depending on where you are in Digital Performer (shortcut: a).

= **I-BEAM TOOL**. Used exclusively for selecting a specific time range (shortcut: i).

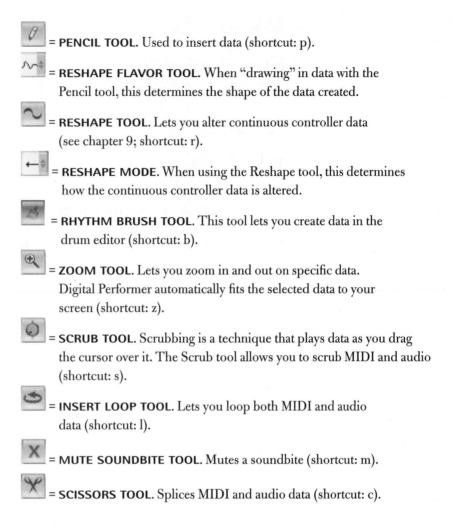

= **PENCIL TOOL.** Used to insert data (shortcut: p).

= **RESHAPE FLAVOR TOOL.** When "drawing" in data with the Pencil tool, this determines the shape of the data created.

= **RESHAPE TOOL.** Lets you alter continuous controller data (see chapter 9; shortcut: r).

= **RESHAPE MODE.** When using the Reshape tool, this determines how the continuous controller data is altered.

= **RHYTHM BRUSH TOOL.** This tool lets you create data in the drum editor (shortcut: b).

= **ZOOM TOOL.** Lets you zoom in and out on specific data. Digital Performer automatically fits the selected data to your screen (shortcut: z).

= **SCRUB TOOL.** Scrubbing is a technique that plays data as you drag the cursor over it. The Scrub tool allows you to scrub MIDI and audio (shortcut: s).

= **INSERT LOOP TOOL.** Lets you loop both MIDI and audio data (shortcut: l).

= **MUTE SOUNDBITE TOOL.** Mutes a soundbite (shortcut: m).

= **SCISSORS TOOL.** Splices MIDI and audio data (shortcut: c).

7.2 Deleting and Moving Notes

Editing is the act of refining a previously recorded performance.

As you move the Marquee cursor around a MIDI track, you will notice that it changes shape, depending upon where it is located. These different shapes indicate that the cursor is ready to perform different editing functions, matched to the current context. For example, when it is not near any notes, the cursor appears as a cross-hair (+). The cross-hair can be used to select several MIDI notes at a time. In figure 7.2, the user dragged the cross-hair cursor to select a group of MIDI notes.

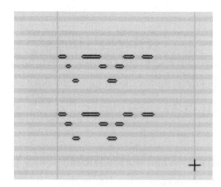

FIGURE 7.2 Cross-Hair Cursor (Marquee Tool) Selects Group of MIDI Notes

When positioned over a note, the cursor appears as an arrow. Clicking the note selects it.

Perhaps the simplest editing procedure is deleting a wrong note. Use the Marquee tool to select the unwanted note, and then hit the Delete key. In figure 7.3, an apparent wrong note is being selected for termination.

FIGURE 7.3 Arrow Cursor (Marquee Tool) Selects Single MIDI Note

Similarly, dragging a selected note will move it, either vertically (changing the pitch) or horizontally (changing the rhythm). To move one note, drag it with the arrow cursor. To move a group of notes, drag the cross-hair over the desired region, and then drag them all as a group to their desired new location.

As you move and select data, you may notice your edits being restricted to a rhythmic grid, such as eighth notes. If this is the case, the "Edit Resolution" button, near the word "Unit," is on. This button will restrict your editing to a set rhythmic value, determined by the neighboring Unit parameter. When Edit Resolution is on, the square appears blue.

Unit = ♩ 4|000 beats

FIGURE 7.4 Edit Resolution Toggle. Controls snap-to-grid resolution, as set in the Unit parameter.

In this case, the rhythmic value is set to "whole notes," meaning the user can only select and move data in four-beat increments. If you are writing loop-based music, you will nearly always want this on. Also, if you are changing the pitch of a note by dragging it vertically, you should have this on. The unit will prevent the note from sliding slightly forward or backward in time, as you change pitch. Of course, there will be times when you desire freedom from the tyranny of the unit grid and will turn it off.

SHORTCUT ▸ Toggle the Edit Resolution behavior by holding down the Command key while editing. Though the icon won't change, its behavior will reverse, for as long as you hold down the Command key.

7.3 Event Information Bar

When you select a MIDI note with the Marquee tool, its properties appear in the Event Information Bar, located to the right of the Quick Filter.

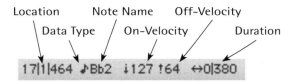

FIGURE 7.5 Event Information Bar

Six properties for this event are shown here.

- **LOCATION** indicates the onset or attack of the pitch, in this case, measure 17, beat 1, tick 464.

- **DATA TYPE**, in this case, a graphical note represents that the event is a MIDI note.

- **NOTE NAME**, in this case, a Bb2. The number indicates the octave, with the lowest octave being 0 and the highest being 7.

- **ON–VELOCITY**. In MIDI, the on-velocity is typically determined by how hard you hit the key on your keyboard. Musically, this most commonly determines the attack quality of the sound. Velocity has a range of 0 to 127. In this case, it is 127, the maximum.

- **OFF–VELOCITY** is determined by how quickly you lift the key.

- **DURATION** determines how long the note is held, consequently determining its release point. In this case, the note is held for 0 beats and 380 ticks—roughly, a dotted eighth note.

If you wish to view additional information in the Event Information Bar, activate it in the Time Formats window, accessible via Studio–Time Formats. Here, "Frames" and "End Time" have been activated.

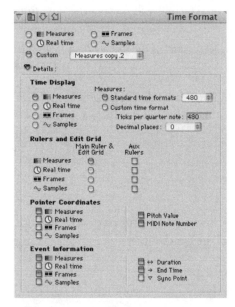

FIGURE 7.6 Time Formats Window

Once you have selected a note, you can alter its properties by clicking on the data in the Event Information Bar, typing a new value, and then Enter.

The Event Information Bar applies to any kind of data in the Sequence Editor, not just MIDI notes. For example, if you are editing foot pedaling, you can click on one Up or Down event, and change its properties in the Event Information Bar.

7.4 Changing Start and End Points

When the cursor is positioned over the beginning or end of a MIDI note, it changes into a hand that lets you quickly change the note's duration. Here, the cursor is placed over the end point of a brass lick in "Upbeat Rock."

FIGURE 7.7 Hand Cursor at Note's End Point

Once the cursor changes into a hand, click and drag to extend or shorten the note's duration.

FIGURE 7.8 Changing a MIDI Note Duration

As with selecting and moving data, this feature will be constrained by the Edit Resolution Toggle's Unit value, when it is activated. As always, the Edit Resolution Toggle can be flipped by holding down the Command key while completing the edit.

When the pointer is placed over the start point, a similar hand appears. This allows you to change the placement of the note's attack.

FIGURE 7.9 Hand Cursor Editing a Note's Start Point

7.5 Scissors

The Scissors tool (shortcut: c) is a convenient way to divide a note into two separate notes. In figure 7.10, there is a whole note in measure 1.

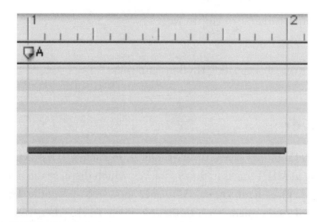

FIGURE 7.10 Whole Note

This can be quickly cut into two half notes with the scissors tool.

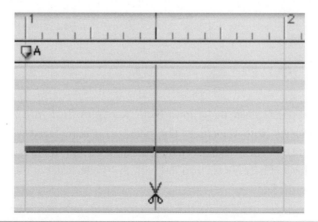

FIGURE 7.11 Scissor Tool Dividing Whole Note into Two Half Notes

If you drag across a note while the Edit Resolution Toggle is on, the Scissors tool will cut the note in whatever increment the Unit value is set to. In figure 7.12, the whole note is quickly cut into a measure of eighth notes.

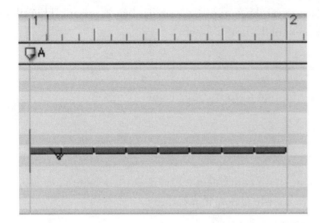

FIGURE 7.12 Whole Note Divided into Eighth Notes

This is a very quick way to create repeating rhythms and rolls.

7.6 Velocity Layer

The Sequence Editor has multiple layers of information on each MIDI track. So far, we have been looking at MIDI tracks in the Note layer, which displays the notes' pitches and their rhythmic placement. Digital Performer shows "Note" in the Track Information Panel, as well as the piano icon to the left of the track, when you are viewing the Notes layer.

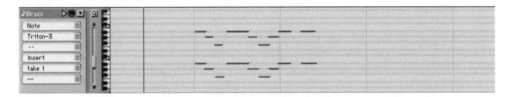

FIGURE 7.13 Note Layer

In addition, there is a separate layer that shows Note Velocities. In figure 7.14, the MIDI Edit row indicates Note Velocities. The piano icon is replaced with a numerical scale going from 0 to 127. Where each note begins and ends, there is a red "V" indicating velocity level. These Vs correspond with the Time Ruler at the top and the 0-to-127 scale on the left.

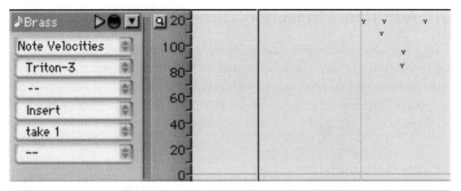

FIGURE 7.14 Note Velocities

How does "velocity" differ from "volume"? *Velocity* is typically determined by how hard you hit the key on your keyboard while recording. Musically, this most directly translates into the accent and tone color of the note. The lowest possible velocity value is 0, while the highest possible velocity value is 127.

While a raise in velocity typically makes a sound louder, *velocity is not volume.* In MIDI, *volume* is the actual loudness of the sound. If you imagine a trumpet player, the tone color of the sound will change substantially as he plays louder. In addition to getting louder, the sound will shift from dark to bright. This tone color change is represented by a change in velocity.

A trumpet patch using high velocity and low volume is like a trumpet player playing loudly from across a football field. The tone color is bright, but the sound itself is soft. Likewise, a trumpet patch using a low velocity with a high volume is like a trumpet player playing quietly while he sits right next to you. The tone color is dark and muted, while the sound itself is loud.

When you are working with a sampler, velocity often determines what sample you hear. In a high-quality sample patch, there are several audio files for each pitch. In the example of a trumpet, they will record a trumpet player playing both loudly and softly. If the velocity value is between 1 and 63, the softer sample will be triggered. If the velocity is between 64 and 127, the louder sample will be triggered.

Sampling patches can get quite complex. For instance, you may have a bass patch that triggers a ghost note when the velocity is from 1 to 10, a sustained note from 11 to 105, and a slide from 106 to 127.

You can edit these velocities the same way you edit notes in the "Note" layer. When you place the cursor directly over a velocity message, the cursor turns into a finger, which acts like the arrow in the Note layer. You can drag velocities vertically. You can also highlight them, and change their properties in the Event Information Bar.

7.7 Additional Selection Techniques

So far, our editing techniques have primarily dealt with altering individual notes. Of course, you can also edit large amounts of MIDI data at once. To do so, you must first select the specific data you wish to edit. Any edit made to one note in the selection will be applied to the entire group. You can also choose from a variety of editing functions in Digital Performer's pull-down menus.

CROSS–HAIR POINTER

As discussed in section 7.2, one way to select a group of MIDI data is by dragging the cross-hair pointer. The cross-hair selects the top layer only. For instance, the following example has a volume layer (diagonal line) in addition to the note layer. Dragging the cross-hair in this layer will only select the note, and not the volume value. (The volume layer is discussed in chapter 11.)

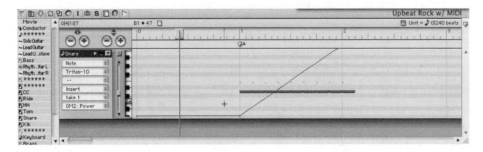

FIGURE 7.15 Selecting with the Cross–Hair

Since only the notes were selected, the volume data remains after we hit Delete.

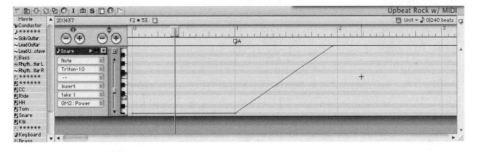

FIGURE 7.16 Volume Curve Remains

The cross-hair cursor can allow us to select large amounts of data, or even the whole track. Just zoom out until all the data is visible on the screen, and then drag from the beginning to the end.

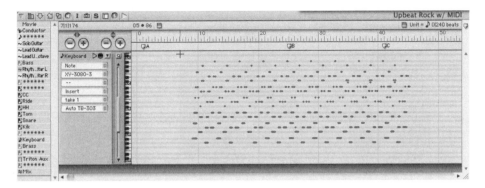

FIGURE 7.17 Select-All Using Cross-Hair. Drag over the region.

DOUBLE-CLICKING ON DATA

However, this can be inconvenient, if you are zoomed in doing detailed editing. It is much more convenient to double-click on any one note. Doing so selects all of the notes in the given track. As with dragging the cross-hair cursor, this selects *only* the notes and not any background layers.

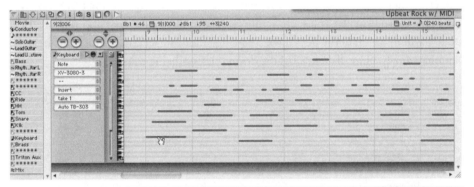

FIGURE 7.18 Select-All Using Pointer. Double-click any note or other MIDI element.

This is also true for other kinds of data. For example, if you are using pitch bend in your track, you can select all of the pitch bends by double-clicking on any one pitch-bend message.

DOUBLE-CLICKING ON THE KEYBOARD ICON

You can also select any one pitch throughout an entire sequence by double-clicking that pitch on the keyboard icon. Here, the middle tom-tom is selected throughout the entire track.

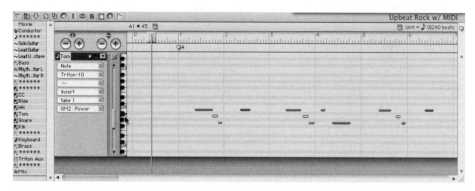

FIGURE 7.19 Selecting All Occurrences of a Note. Double-clicking a note on the keyboard icon selects all occurrences of that note throughout the sequence.

Again, this technique selects only notes, not any background layers.

LASSO

The Marquee tool can also display as a lasso cursor ![lasso icon]. The lasso allows you to select data over multiple MIDI tracks. As you may have noticed, when you drag the cross-hair cursor above or below the track, the Sequence Editor responds by scrolling that particular track up or down. If you are using the lasso cursor, the cursor will move on to the next track, allowing you to select data on multiple tracks simultaneously. Here, data in all of the drum tracks is being selected.

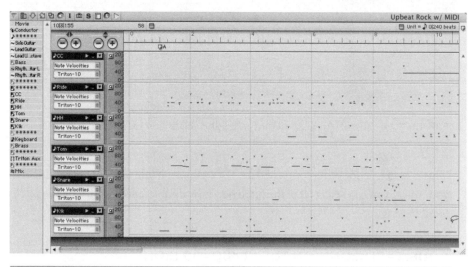

FIGURE 7.20 The Lasso Selects across Tracks.

In many layers, such as Note Velocities and Volume, the default cursor is the Lasso. In the Note layer, you can get the Lasso cursor by holding down Control-Option.

As with the other Marquee tool selections, this selects only the top layer.

I-BEAM

The I-Beam tool can be used to select all of the data on one track, across all layers. Its keyboard shortcut is "I." Here, the I-Beam is being used to select our snare roll and volume crescendo.

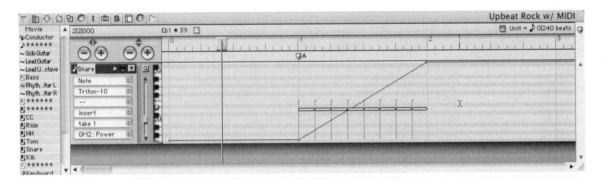

FIGURE 7.21 The I-Beam Selects All Layers

When we hit Delete, the notes are gone, and so is the volume data.

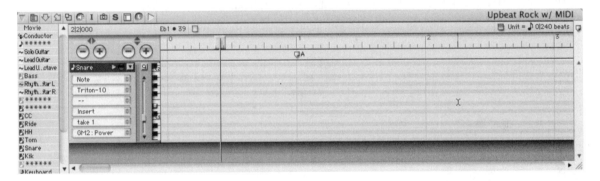

FIGURE 7.22 All Layers Deleted

The selection you make with your I-Beam cursor can be expanded to other tracks by shift-clicking on the other tracks.

Clicking the I-Beam inside a track places a blinking cursor called the "insertion point." Later, when we copy and paste, pasting will place data at this point. Here, the cursor has been placed at beat 3 of measure 0.

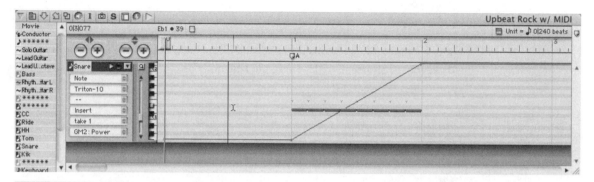

FIGURE 7.23 Insertion Point

You can move the insertion point around with the Tab key. Typing Tab will move it forward to the next MIDI event. In this case, Tabbing once would move it to measure 1, where the first snare hit is located. Tabbing a second time would move it on to the next snare hit, at measure 1, beat 1, tick 240. Option-Tab moves the insertion point backwards.

Shift-Tab will select everything between the present location of the insertion point and the next MIDI event. In the following example, typing Tab moved the insertion point to measure 1. Shift-Tab was then typed four times to select the first four eighth notes.

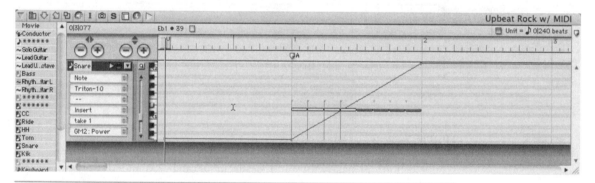

FIGURE 7.24 Selecting Data with Shift-Tab and the I-Beam.

Similarly, you can move the insertion point to the beginning of the sequence by pressing Return. Option-Return sends the insertion point to the end of the sequence. As with the Tab key, Shift-Return will select everything from the current position to the beginning of the sequence, and Option-Shift-Return selects to the end.

TIME RULER SELECTING

When you place the cursor over the Time Ruler, it automatically changes into an I-Beam cursor. When you drag across the Time Ruler, Digital Performer selects all data on visible tracks over that time period. Here, all of measure 1 is being selected for the drum tracks.

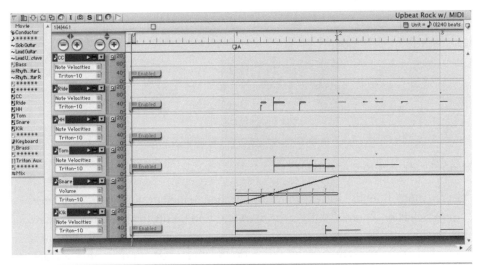

FIGURE 7.25 Selecting from the Time Ruler

As with other I-Beam selections, this selects the material on all layers in the Sequence Editor.

SELECTION DRAWER

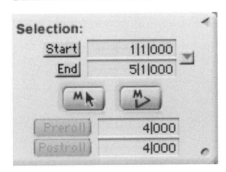

FIGURE 7.26 The Selection Drawer

The Control Panel's Selection drawer allows you to select regions by typing values, rather than using a graphic tool. You can also use it to expand and manipulate your selections and also link your selections to playback. When you make a selection with the I-Beam tool, your selection is reflected in the Selection drawer's Start and End times.

In figure 7.26, a selection has been made from measure 1 to 5. You can expand this selection in a variety of ways. Perhaps the most useful is "Set to Chunk Bounds," found in the Selection mini-menu, which can be accessed by clicking on the upside-down triangle ▼.

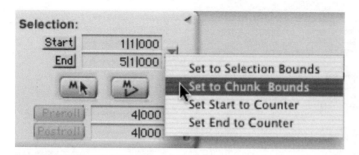

FIGURE 7.27 Set to Chunk Bounds

"Set to Chunk Bounds" will expand your selection to include your entire sequence. "Set to Selection Bounds" will set the Start and End points to a selection made by the cross-hair or lasso cursor. "Set Start/End to Counter" are also available, but it is much more convenient to simply click on the "Start" or "End" buttons, which achieve the same result.

Digital Performer also allows you to affect playback with your selections. When "Memory Play" is on, two arrows appear in the Sequence Editor. When you click Play, playback will begin at the first arrow and end at the second.

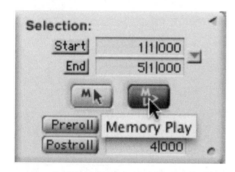

FIGURE 7.28 Memory Play

When you activate "Link Selection to Playback," whatever you select in the Sequence Editor will be imported into the Memory Play settings. In this manner, you can highlight the portion of the sequence you wish to listen to and click Play. Only your selection will play back. In figure 7.29, the user selected measures 1 through 5 for playback.

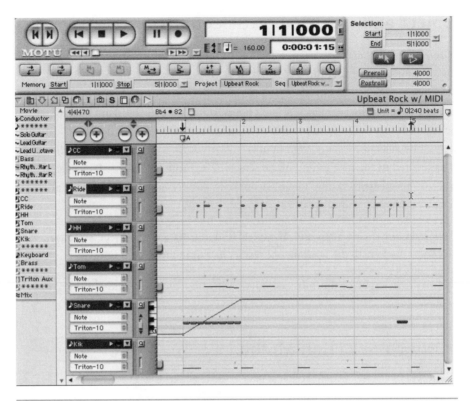

FIGURE 7.29 Playback Selection Measures 1 to 5

You can also activate a "preroll" and "postroll." Here, each setting is activated and set to four beats. Digital Performer will begin playback four beats before the start time in Memory Play and end four beats after the end time in Memory Play.

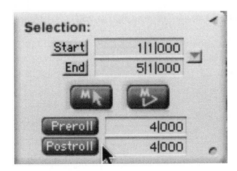

FIGURE 7.30 Preroll and Postroll

SELECT ALL

As with many programs, Digital Performer provides a Select All feature (shortcut: Command–a) in the Edit menu. This will select all material on all tracks throughout your entire sequence. If, at some point, you wish to remove your selection, you can use Deselect (shortcut: Command-d) in the Edit menu.

Object and Time-Range Selections

There are two primary types of selections in Digital Performer: an object selection and a time-range selection. An *object selection* selects specific data events. The selections made from figures 7.15 to 7.20 are object selections, where the data events are notes. Since we are selecting only notes, other data in the same location is not selected. A *time-range selection* selects a particular time range, rather than particular data. The selections made from figures 7.21 to 7.25 are time-range selections. All data located in the time range will be selected, including all layers. However, data is not a prerequisite for a time-range selection. In fact, a time-range selection can occur over a completely empty measure.

Any selection made with the Marquee tool results in an object selection. Any selection made with the I-Beam tool results in a time-range selection.

Let's review eight of the most common selection methods and the best way to achieve them.

Which Selection Method

Desire 1:	Select a region of data in the top layer only.
Example:	You wish to highlight a particular keyboard lick so that you can transpose it up an octave.
Best Way:	Drag using the Marquee Tool.
Desire 2:	Select a region of data in all layers.
Example:	You wish to highlight a snare roll and its crescendo so you can copy and paste it to a timpani track.
Best Way:	Drag using the I-Beam tool.
Desire 3:	Select a region of data in the top layer only, and over multiple tracks.
Example:	You wish to highlight a crescendo happening on multiple tracks so you can delete it without deleting the notes.
Best Way:	Using the lasso cursor, drag over multiple tracks. If you are in the "Note" layer, hold down Control-Option for the lasso to appear.
Desire 4:	Select a region of data in all layers, and over a specific group of tracks.
Example:	You decide to remove keyboards and guitar from your introduction, leaving only bass and drums.
Best Way:	Using the I-Beam tool, make the selection on one track. Then Shift-click on the other tracks to expand the selection.

Desire 5:	Select a region of data in all layers, and over all tracks.
Example:	You wish to get rid of verse 3 entirely.
Best Way:	Place the cursor over the Time Ruler until the I-Beam appears, then drag.
Desire 6:	Select every instance of one kind of data throughout an entire track.
Example:	You wish to select all the notes in the bass part in order to transpose them up an octave.
Best Way:	Double-click on any instance of that data type.
Desire 7:	Select one pitch throughout the entire track.
Example:	You wish to select all the snare drum hits in a full drum track so that you can transpose them to a different sample, such as a hand clap.
Best Way:	Double-click on that pitch in the Pitch Ruler.
Desire 8:	Select all layers of one track throughout the entire sequence.
Example:	You wish to delete entirely your keyboard part's data.
Best Way 1:	Type Command-a (Select All). This will set the selection bounds to the entire sequence. Then click the name of the track you wish to highlight.
Best Way 2:	Using the I-Beam tool, place the insertion point on the track. Type Return, sending it to the beginning. Then type Option-Shift-Return, selecting everything to the end.

7.8 Copy/Cut/Paste/Merge

In Digital Performer, the Copy/Cut/Paste functions work just as they do in basic word-processing programs. The Copy and Cut commands place whatever material is selected into the clipboard. Paste takes the material from the clipboard and inserts it at whichever measure is highlighted, or at the insertion point.

You have several ways to copy and paste in Digital Performer. Begin by selecting the material you wish to copy/paste. Then:

OPTION A.

1. Hold Option. The cursor turns from a hand with one pointed finger to a hand with two pointed fingers.

2. Drag the selected material to its new location.

OPTION B.

1. Choose Edit–Copy (or Cut).

2. Click the I-Beam where you wish to paste the material.

3. Choose Edit–Paste.

OPTION C.

1. Type Command-c.

2. Click the I-Beam where you wish to paste the material.

3. Type Command-v.

I find option A to be the most versatile.

When you are making your initial selection, be aware of whether you are selecting the top layer only or all of the layers. This will make a difference in what material is pasted. Also, it is recommended that you use time-range selections when copying. For instance, if you wish to copy and paste one measure of your keyboard part, and that measure begins with an eighth-note rest, you must copy this rest along with the ensuing notes. Only a time-range selection will allow you to do so.

If you choose "Paste," any existing material at the new location will be deleted. Let's imagine you have a volume fade at measure 4 of the piano part. Then you copy measure 4 of the Rhodes part—which is only notes—and paste it into measure 4 of the piano. When you complete the paste, the previous volume fade will be deleted. If you wish to keep that volume fade, choose Edit–Merge (or Command-m). This acts similarly to Paste but does not erase the material previously located on the track. In a sense, Merge functions like overdub recording. The Option-drag method acts like Merge.

7.9 Loops

Loops are prominent in today's music industry, and they are easy to create in Digital Performer. Let's consider the drum elements in our "Upbeat Rock" track. Let's say that we decide to make a loop out of the first measure, repeating it for seven measures, followed by a fill. This could be created in several ways.

We could copy and paste the material, for the first seven measures. In addition to the techniques discussed in the previous section, Digital Performer also provides a Repeat command in the Edit menu (shortcut: Command-r), which allows you to quickly paste a selection multiple times.

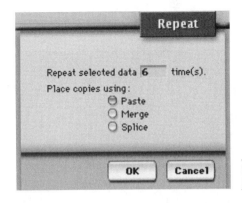

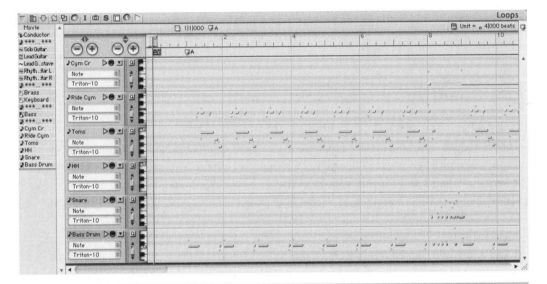

FIGURE 7.31 Repeat. Access via Edit–Repeat (shortcut: Command-r).

Using either of these techniques, our file would look like figure 7.32.

FIGURE 7.32 Drum Loop Viewed in Sequence Editor.

While this works, it has a downside. If you desire to make a change, you have to make the change to every measure or complete the copy and paste all over again. Fortunately, Digital Performer provides a Loop tool in the Tools Palette (shortcut: l). To loop material, drag over it with the Loop tool. This will create a loop that is placed on a new Loop layer. Most likely, you will have to adjust the length of the loops. You can do so by highlighting the bottom left corner of the loop, and then changing the "Repeat Times" portion of the Event Information Bar.

With this technique, our file looks like figure 7.33. In this case, if we make a change to measure 1, it will also affect all of the subsequent loops played in measures 2 through 7.

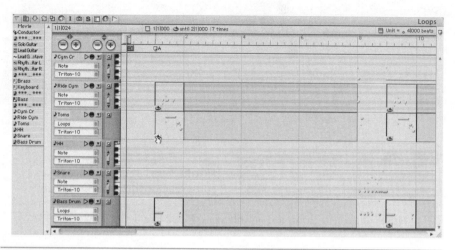

FIGURE 7.33 The Loop Tool

Loops can also be accomplished quickly by selecting the material you wish to loop and choosing Region–Set Loop.

7.10 Quantize

Once you have material selected, you can alter it in a variety of ways using commands from the Region and Edit menus. Quantize is one such command. Quantizing is a means to modify a performance rhythmically. When you quantize a performance, all the notes will be moved directly onto or closer to a strict rhythmic pattern. If you perform a note slightly after the beat, quantizing it will move it exactly on the beat.

Digital Performer divides the sequence rhythmically into measures, beats, and ticks. Ticks are a subdivision of the beat, and Digital Performer defaults to 480 ticks per quarter note. Therefore, the second eighth note of the beat would fall on tick 240. The fourth sixteenth note would fall on tick 360.

	Beat 1					Beat 2
Quarter Notes	0					480 (0)
Eighth Notes	0			240		480 (0)
Swing Eighths	0				320	480 (0)
Triplets	0		160		320	480 (0)
Sixteenths	0	120		240	360	480 (0)
Sixteenth Triplets	0	80	160	240	320	400	480 (0)

FIGURE 7.34 Quantization: Note Values and Ticks

Quantize your performance by selecting a region and choosing Region–Quantize (shortcut: Command-0), which invokes the Quantize window. Usually, you'll want to quantize "Notes and Soundbites" and "Attacks," as shown here.

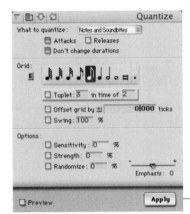

FIGURE 7.35 Quantize Window

The Grid setting determines what rhythmic value the music is moved to. In this case, it is set to eighth notes, which means every attack will be moved to either tick 0 or tick 240, thus falling exactly on one of the eighth notes in the measure. As a general rule of thumb, you should set the Grid value to the smallest rhythmic subdivision in the music. If there are no sixteenths, and eighths are the smallest value, then an eighth-note grid will do. If there are sixteenth notes in the music, this rhythmic subdivision will be destroyed if you quantize to anything larger than sixteenths. In the case of our "Upbeat Rock" tune, the smallest rhythmic value is eighth notes, so we can quantize to eighths.

In this window, the "Tuplet" feature lets you quantize to triplets or other polyrhythms. "Swing" lets you quantize to swing rhythms. Notice that both triplets and swing eighths will move attacks to tick 0 and 320. However, tick 160 is included in triplets but omitted in swing eighths.

"UPBEAT ROCK" QUANTIZED TO EIGHTHS

Let's quantize the "Upbeat Rock" keyboard part. In the following file, the keyboard part has been quantized to straight eighth notes—which is what the part calls for. Notice how every attack is exactly on tick 000 or 240, on the Event List shown in figure 7.36.

TRACK 5

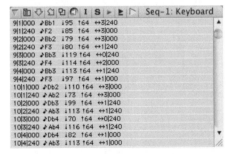

FIGURE 7.36 Quantized as Eighths

As with the conductor track, it shows a list of all the events on the track. The left-most column is the location of the event—in this case, the attack of the note. For instance, the first attack in the example above is at 9 | 1 | 000, the second at 9 | 1 | 240, and so on.

"UPBEAT ROCK" QUANTIZED TO HALF NOTES

It is possible to completely destroy your part with the wrong quantize settings. In our keyboard part, the shortest rhythmic value is eighth notes. If we quantized to half notes, the eighth-note pattern would be destroyed, because each note would be moved to the nearest half note. In figure 7.37, notice how every note is moved to beat 1 or 3.

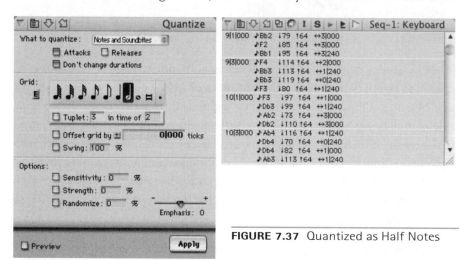

TRACK 6

FIGURE 7.37 Quantized as Half Notes

"UPBEAT ROCK" QUANTIZED TO SWING EIGHTHS

Next, we'll try quantizing to swing eighths. This will move each attack to either tick 0, 160, or 320. In this case, the musical effect is not particularly desired, as "Upbeat Rock" now sounds like Little Red Riding Hood skipping through the forest, but the quantizing was successful, nonetheless.

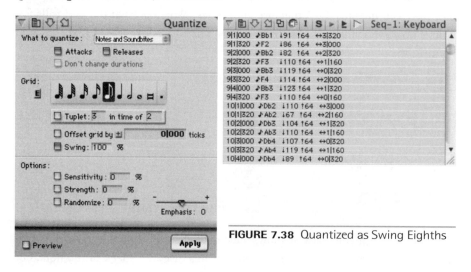

TRACK 7

FIGURE 7.38 Quantized as Swing Eighths

Notice the Percentage option, next to Swing. This determines how much the eighths are swung. Straight eighths fall at 0 and 240. Swing eighths, at 100%, fall at 0 and 320. Notice that the difference between straight and swung is 80 ticks. If you place the swing percentage at 50%, this difference will be cut in half to 40, resulting in attacks placed at 0 and 280.

Rhythmic Subdivision	Beat 1		Beat 2
Straight Eighth Notes	0	240	0
50% Swing Eighth Notes	0	280	0
100% Swing Eighth Notes	0	320	0

FIGURE 7.39 Swing Percentages

RANDOMIZE

So far, quantizing has resulted in everything being placed *exactly* on the beat. This is not ideal, mainly because humans do not perform perfectly. A certain margin of error is human, and it sounds good.

This is what the Randomize function is for. When turned on, the notes will be moved randomly left and right after they are quantized. Rather than all of the attacks ending up exactly at tick 0 and 240, they will be somewhere near the beat, such as 470–010 and 230–250. The range of the margin of error is determined by how high the Randomize Percentage is set.

The Emphasis feature systematically moves attacks earlier or later during the randomize process. There is still a margin of error, but the range is moved forward or backward. Rather than a range of 230 to 250, around 240, it would become 220–240. Notice, in the following example, that attacks are randomized, but they fall consistently before the beat.

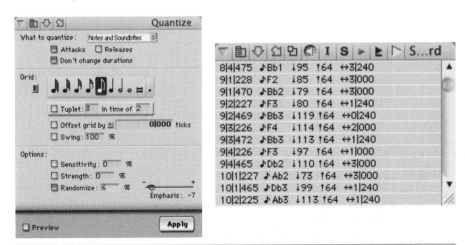

FIGURE 7.40 Quantization, Randomized with Emphasis Before the Beat

SENSITIVITY AND STRENGTH

The Strength feature allows you to move a performance a percentage of the way to the beat. Let's say you have a blues pianist play a keyboard part, and he is playing everything laid back. For instance, one particular downbeat is played at tick 034 instead of 000. You want to clean him up a bit, rhythmically, but without destroying his feel. Standard quantizing would destroy his feel by placing everything exactly on the beat. Randomize would also destroy his feel. While the attacks would not fall on the beat, their margin of error would be genuinely random and not based on the original performance. Quantizing with Strength will result in an imperfect performance, but the imperfections will be based on the original performance. If the Strength is at 50%, each attack would shift halfway to the beat, thus cleaning up the performance, but keeping a portion of the original feel. In the case of our blues player, whose downbeat fell at 034, quantizing with Strength at 50% would place the attack at 017.

Sensitivity allows you to quantize only a portion of the measure. For instance, if you quantize to quarter notes with sensitivity at 50%, the 50% of the measure closest to each quarter will be quantized. Everything else will be left alone.

GROOVE QUANTIZE

Groove Quantizing is a means of quantizing to a pattern other than the strict, mathematical division of the beat. For instance, rather than quantizing to 0, 120, 240, and 360 (sixteenths notes), you could quantize to 0, 130, 260, and 370. Groove quantizing can also affect velocities and durations.

Digital Performer provides some groove patterns for you called "DNA grooves." To use them, select the material you wish to quantize and choose Region–Groove Quantize.

FIGURE 7.41 Groove Quantize Window

In the Groove Quantize window, select a groove to use. If you wish to view and edit the pattern, click on the Edit button.

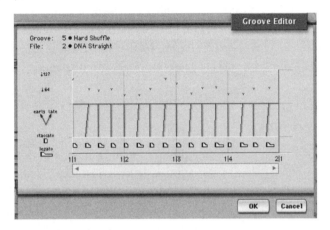

FIGURE 7.42 Editing the "Hard Shuffle" Groove Quantization Template

Here, you can see the "Hard Shuffle" groove. You can see that every other sixteenth is late—some later than others. Also notice there is a specific velocity pattern, placing accents on the first beat and around beat 3. If you desire, you can make changes by dragging the different aspects in this window.

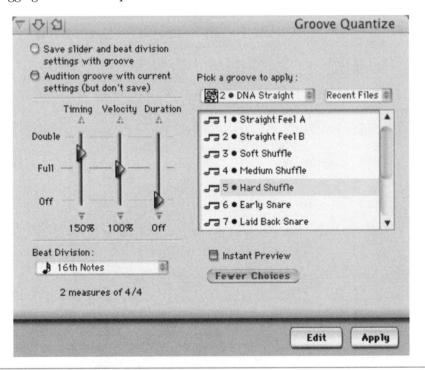

FIGURE 7.43 Groove Quantization: More Choices

Also, notice the "More Choices" button in the Groove Quantize window. Here, you can set the percentages for the timing, velocity, and duration of the groove. In the example above, the velocity is at 100%, meaning that the pattern in the groove will be applied exactly. The duration is at 0% (or Off), so the durations will not be changed. The timing is at 150%. This means the lateness of the groove will be exaggerated. For instance, if a certain sixteenth note is 30 ticks late in the groove pattern, quantizing to 150% will make it 45 ticks late.

CREATING GROOVES

You can create your own grooves based on an original musical performance. For instance, let's say you lay down a hi-hat track that you just love. Digital Performer allows you to create a groove based on this performance, including the timing, velocity, and durations. There are two reasons you may wish to do this. First, it would allow you to easily replicate the feel in other sequences. Second, it would allow you to quantize other elements to this groove. Rather then quantizing your bass and keyboards to the strict, mathematical grid, you would essentially be quantizing them to the hi-hats.

To create a groove, highlight the material you want to be its basis, and choose Region–Create Groove.

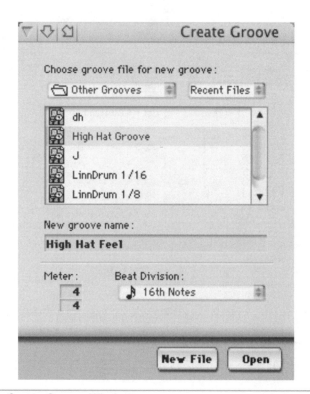

FIGURE 7.44 Create Groove Window

It is logical to store your original grooves in the "Other Grooves" folder. Once you modify an existing groove file or create a new one, you can save your groove. After your groove is created, you can use it just as you would use the DNA grooves.

7.11 Change Duration

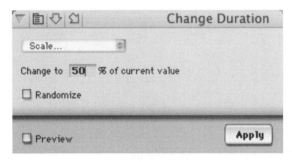

FIGURE 7.45 Change Duration Menu

Also in the Region menu is a "Change Duration" feature. This uniformly changes a group of durations to other durations, like transforming a group of notes to be twice as fast. When you Choose Region–Change Duration, there are several options.

SET   Assigns all selected notes a specific duration.

ADD   Adds a specific amount to each duration.

SUBTRACT Subtracts a specific amount from each duration.

SCALE   Multiplies each duration by a percentage, making them all proportionally longer or shorter.

LIMIT   Limits selected notes to a specified range.

MOVE RELEASES is a particularly useful option. It changes the duration of each note so that it ends at the exact time another note begins. The release point of each note is moved forward or backward to the closest attack point of another note. The end result is a completely smooth performance, with no breaks in between the notes.

Below is a variation of the keyboard part from "Upbeat Rock." Notice how some notes are short and staccato, while other notes are longer and overlap.

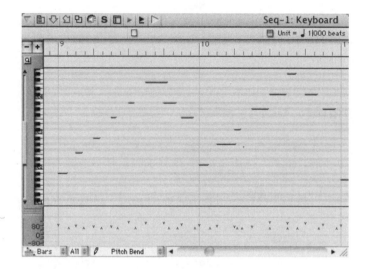

FIGURE 7.46 Before "Move Releases" Is Applied

After changing the durations with Move Releases, the performance becomes entirely seamless.

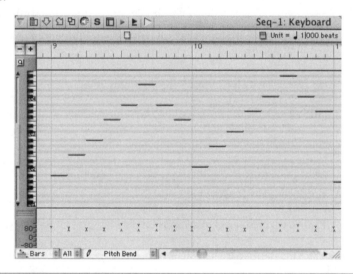

FIGURE 7.47 After "Move Releases" Is Applied to Fig. 7.46.

This is particularly useful when getting rid of unwanted overlap in a performance. For example, overlapped notes in the bass part muddy up the part and the mix. This is a quick way to get rid of them.

EXTENDED RELEASES is similar. However, the duration will always be lengthened and never shortened. With Move Releases, some durations are actually shortened to get to the closest attack point, such as the note starting on the upbeat of measure 9, beat 3. With Extend Releases, this note would be lengthened, resulting in a quarter note.

7.12 Transpose

Using the Transpose command in the Region menu, you can change the pitch of your performance. Simply highlight the material you wish to transpose, and choose Region–Transpose (shortcut: Command-9).

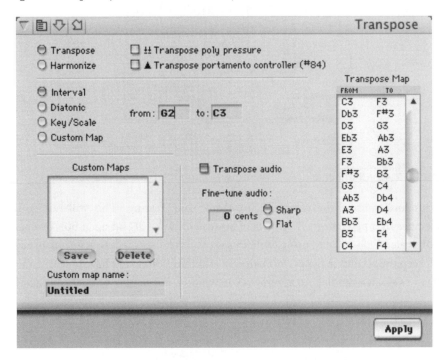

FIGURE 7.48 Transpose Window

Figure 7.48 shows the Transpose window. Currently, it is set to transpose, not harmonize. If set to "Harmonize," Digital Performer would create intervals. For instance, if you select a C and transpose it up a perfect fifth, you get a G. If you select the same C and harmonize it up a perfect fifth, you would get both the C and the G.

Also, notice that it is currently set to transpose by an interval, and it is set to transpose from G2 to C3. These specific note names do not matter; rather, it is the interval relationship between them that matters. Everything selected will be transposed up a perfect fourth. You would get the same result if you transposed from A2 to D3, or from C#5 to F#5, etc.

7.13 Change Velocity

Also in the Region menu, you can change the velocities in a variety of ways. To uniformly raise the velocities, use the Add feature. Here, you can raise all velocities by a specific amount. In figure 7.49, we are adding 25 to each velocity selected.

WARNING: Be careful using this when your velocities are already high. If you have a performance whose velocities range from 105 to 125, and you add 25 to all of them, each velocity will end up at 127 since this is the highest possible value. In the process, any accents or inflection in the performance will be lost!

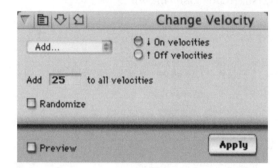

FIGURE 7.49 Change Velocities Window. Adding to the selected velocities.

To uniformly lower the velocities, use the "Scale" feature. This will reduce the velocities by a percentage. A velocity of 80 scaled 75% will end up at 60. A velocity of 36 scaled 75% will end up at 27. In this way, all velocities will be lowered, but you will keep the accents in the performance. In addition, you do not have to worry about all your velocities ending up at zero, as you would if it was the Subtract command.

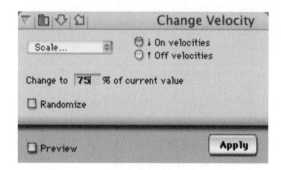

FIGURE 7.50 Change Velocities Window. Scaling the selected velocities.

The other commands available to change velocity are:

SET Sets the velocity of all selected notes to a specific value.

LIMIT Limits the velocities to a specific range. You may wish to use this if you are using a sampler where different velocities trigger different samples—and you wish to avoid particular ones. In the bass example mentioned earlier, to avoid any ghost notes, we would limit velocities to 11–127 (see page 76).

COMPRESS Lowers the velocities of the highest notes, while leaving the lowest notes alone. This is useful if you have a few notes that stick out more than you desire. The *threshold* is the point at which velocities begin to be compressed. If your threshold is 75, all velocities below 75 will not change, while all above 75 will be compressed. The *ratio* determines how much the affected velocities are lowered. With a threshold of 75 and ratio of 3:1, a velocity of 90 will be moved to 80—67% of the way to the threshold. The *gain* allows you to raise all velocities, including those below the threshold, after the compression is complete.

SMOOTH   Allows you to create crescendos and decrescendos (great for snare rolls, timpani rolls, etc.).

7.14 Undo History

With all these tools to edit our music, what if we royally mess it up and want to revert to a previous version of the file? Thankfully, Digital Performer keeps track of our edits and lets us revert to previous versions of our file. To view your edits, choose Edit–Undo History.

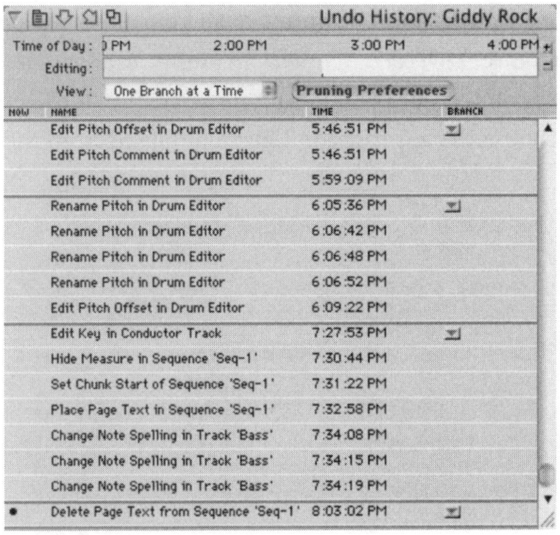

FIGURE 7.51 Undo History Window

The Undo History lists all your edits and the time you made the edit. The Name column on the left indicates which version of the file you are currently using. In this case, we may wish to revert to the "Edit Marker in Sequence 'Upbeat Rock'" made at 12:00:55 p.m. To do so, double-click in its Now column.

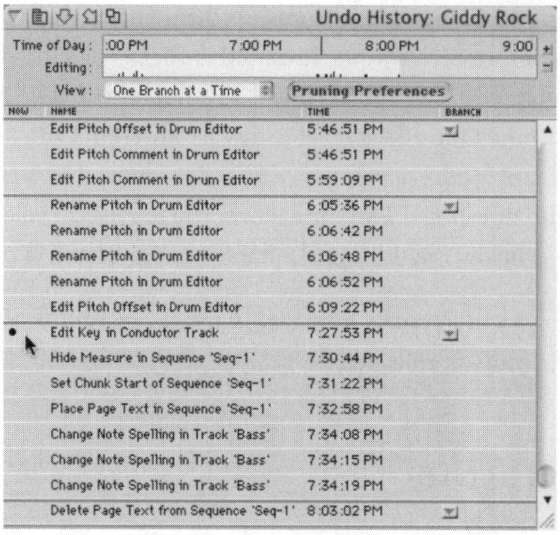

FIGURE 7.52 Changing the Current File Version

As Digital Performer saves all your edits, it is keeping track of a lot of information. This means the size of your Project folder could get larger than you need it to be, especially if your file has a lot of audio. To reduce the size of your project folder, you can "Flush" the undo history. This will remove all your other versions of your file and any data they require. *However, you will no longer be able to revert to previous versions.* If you are absolutely sure you do not need the previous versions stored in the Undo History, choose the appropriate Flush command from the Undo History mini-menu.

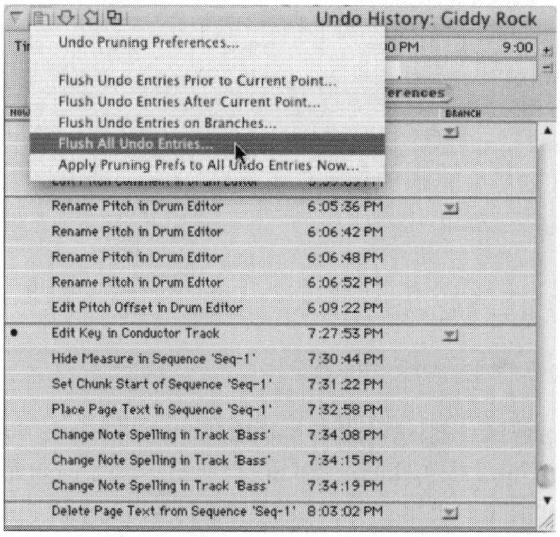

FIGURE 7.53 Flushing Undo History

EDITING WINDOWS

In addition to the Sequence Editor, Digital Performer provides several other editing windows. Truth be told, you will be able to complete almost all of your tasks in the Sequence Editor. While these windows won't give you additional musical capabilities, they do present the information in a different manner, to facilitate different editing approaches. You may feel more comfortable working with the material in one window rather than another. Try them all, and use whichever one you are most comfortable with.

All of these editing windows can be opened from the Sequence Editor's mini-menu. Highlight the track name of the track you wish to edit, and then choose the desired editing window.

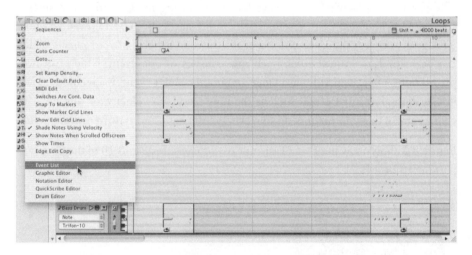

FIGURE 8.1 Choosing Editing Windows from Sequence Editor Mini-Menu

In addition, most of the editing windows can be opened from the Control Panel's Windows drawer. Highlight the track you wish to edit, and click on the appropriate editing icon. Like the other drawers, this can be opened by clicking on the triangle in the upper-right corner of the Control Panel.

FIGURE 8.2 Windows Drawer

= Event List Editor

= Graphic Editor

= Drum Editor

= Quickscribe Editor

FIGURE 8.3 Icons for Editing Windows

8.1 Event List

The Event List is a window we have looked at during the Quantize section (see chapter 7). The Event List presents all the information about MIDI events as text. This gives you very precise control over the different aspects of your music, which can be helpful for critical edits. Each row consists of one event, which can be a played note, a tempo or volume change, or another MIDI event. Each column gives information about that event, such as the note name, on-velocity, or duration. To change any of this information, double-click on the item, and type in the new value.

Figure 8.4 shows how the Event List appears for measures 9 and 10 of the keyboard part in "Upbeat Rock."

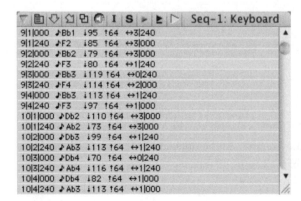

FIGURE 8.4 Event List

8.2 Graphic Editor

The Graphics Editor gives a magnified view of a MIDI or Conductor track. It is the window I most recommend using in conjunction with the Sequence Editor. Each Graphic Editor looks and acts very much like the corresponding track in the Sequence editor, so it is not entirely foreign territory; the Graphic Editor just shows greater detail and a larger workspace. It can be opened easily from the Sequence Editor by holding Command while choosing the track from the Sequence Name menu in the Title Bar. Here, we are opening the Keyboard track for "Upbeat Rock." (Remember to hold down Command when you choose from this menu.)

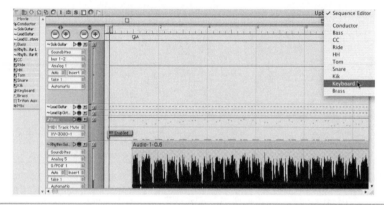

FIGURE 8.5 Choosing a Track for the Graphics Window. Hold Command while you make your selection.

When you are done editing, you can return to the Sequence Editor from the Graphic Editor by choosing Sequence Editor from this menu.

Figure 8.6 shows the Graphic Editor window for our "Upbeat Rock" keyboard part.

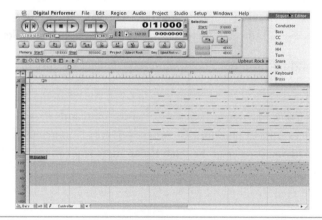

FIGURE 8.6 The Graphic Editor for the Keyboard Track. Returning to the Sequence Editor.

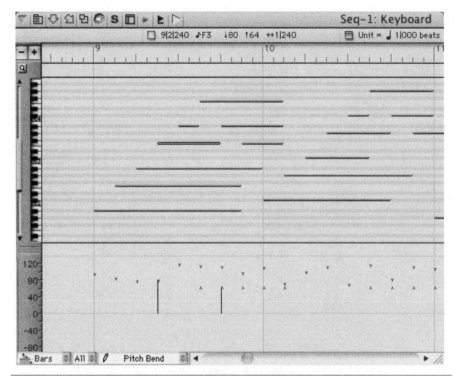

FIGURE 8.7 Graphic Editor for the Keyboard Track

The biggest advantage here over the Sequence Editor is that velocities and controller data are not placed in the same region as the notes. This makes them much easier to see and edit. The bottom half of the screen is dedicated to additional data, besides notes, such as velocity, pitch bend, and volume changes. (Volume and other continuous controllers are covered in chapter 11.) In figure 8.7, you can see the V markings, which are located directly beneath that onset of each note.

At the top of the window is a horizontal timeline in measures and beats. As in the Sequence Editor, each horizontal line on this "piano roll" represents a note. The line's location corresponds with the attack time, release time, and resulting duration. Its vertical placement indicates pitch—corresponding to the Pitch Ruler.

To zoom in and out, use the Zoom buttons located just to the left of the timeline.

As in the Sequence Editor, Command- → and Command- ← act as keyboard shortcuts for zoom. In addition, Command- ↑ and Command- ↓ will zoom vertically, changing the size of the Pitch Ruler. Also, you can use the Zoom tool from the Tools window (shortcut: z).

As with the Sequence Editor, the specific properties of any given event are shown in the Event Information Bar. In figure 8.7, a note is selected. We are given its values: a start time of 9|2|240, the note name F3, on-velocity of 80, off-velocity of 64, and duration of 1|240. If you are unsure what a piece of data means, there is a legend located in the mini-menu.

The Graphic Editor also has an Edit Resolution button ⬚ Unit = ♩ 1|000 beats . Its function is the same as in the Sequence Editor. As with all grids in Digital Performer, you can toggle it on and off by holding down the Command key when you drag.

To view more than one track simultaneously, use the Expand button ▢ in the title bar. This displays a list of all your MIDI tracks on the left. The data for any highlighted track will show up in the editor. In the following graphic, we are viewing the bass and keyboard for "Upbeat Rock."

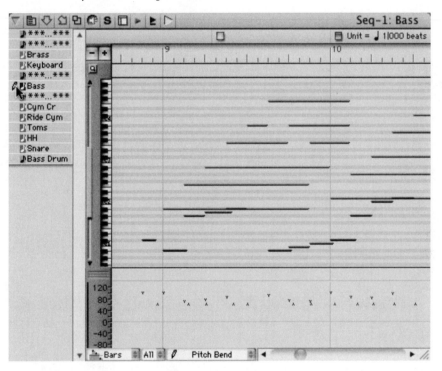

FIGURE 8.8 Bass and Keyboard in Graphic Editor

This is one reason why it is important to name your tracks when you are setting up your file. If we had not done so, our Expand column would read Track-1, Track-2, Track-3, and so on. Being able to identify tracks quickly saves you time in the long run.

Notice that only the velocities for the bass are shown. Though you can display the notes for several instruments at a time, only one instrument's velocity values display. This is controlled by the pencil icon that appears next to the Bass track in the Track

Selector section ⌀🅑Bass . To switch the track displaying velocity information, click to the left of that desired track.

Selecting data here is similar to selecting it in the Sequence Editor. Moving the cursor around MIDI data will produce the cross-hair, arrow, and hand cursors. You can also select data by dragging in the timeline, double-clicking on the Pitch Ruler, or double-clicking on a note.

Also, Option-drag acts as a shortcut for Copy and Paste, in the Graphic Editor.

8.3 Drum Editor

The Drum Editor shares many characteristics of the Graphic Editor.

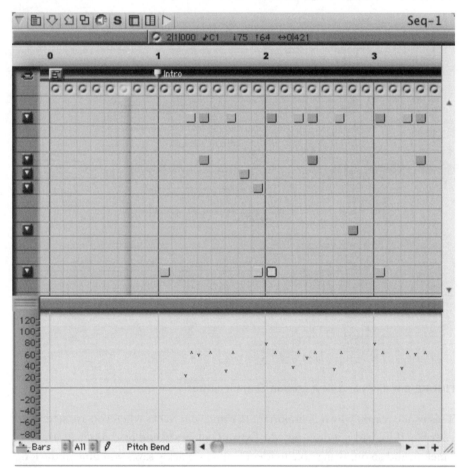

FIGURE 8.9 Drum Editor

As you can see here, the Drum Editor also has a timeline at the top. The Drum Editor utilizes a grid, but the grid is visually represented for you. In this case, the grid is set to eighth notes. As usual, selecting material will be limited to this grid unless you hold the Command key when you edit. As with other windows, the grid can be changed by zooming in and out with the Zoom tool or the keyboard shortcuts Command- ← and Command- →. As with the Graphic Editor, the specific information about a particular event is shown at the top when that event is highlighted.

The Drum Editor also allows you to show and hide tracks by highlighting them in the Expand ▣ section. It also shows velocities at the bottom. The velocities shown (in this case, for the "Ride Cym" track) are those of the track indicated by a pencil icon, in the Expand section.

In the title bar, the Drum Editor has a ▣ Show/Hide Track Information button. This opens a new section that displays vital properties of each track.

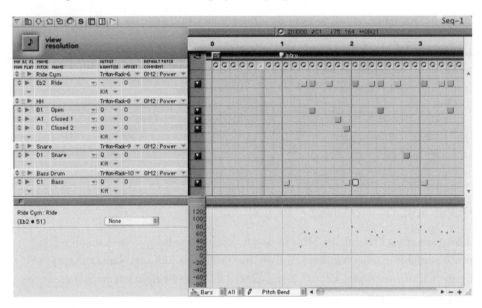

FIGURE 8.10 Track Information in the Drum Editor

The Track Information section provides detailed information about each track, including some very convenient options unique to the Drum Editor.

First, it displays the basic information of each track. For the hi-hat track in "Upbeat Rock," this information is:

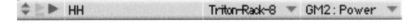

FIGURE 8.11 Track Name in Drum Editor

This section is structured in columns, with each column allowing you to set a particular property.

= Move. Allows you to rearrange tracks vertically.

= Record Enable

= Play Enable

HH = Track Name

Triton-Rack-8 ▼ = MIDI Output

GM2 : Power ▼ = MIDI Patch

FIGURE 8.12 Drum Editor Track Information Properties

As in the Sequence Editor, you can use Option-click to change the track name.

In figure 8.13, you have an individual track for each pitch you have used. This is particularly handy for drum programming, because each individual pitch is a new instrument. In the case of our hi-hats, this information is:

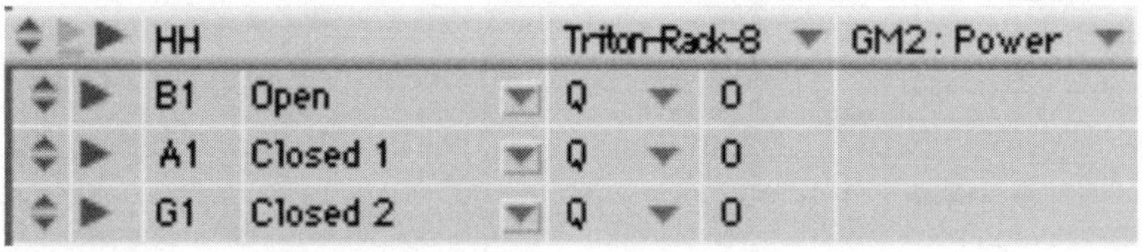

FIGURE 8.13 Pitches Mapped as Drum Names

This gives you a Play-Enable/Mute button for each individual pitch—something that is not available in other windows. You are also given an additional Name column—in figure 8.13 named Open, Closed 1, and Closed 2. At the far right is a field where you can place comments.

The Drum Editor also gives you precise control over timing. To the left of the Comments is an "offset" feature, allowing you to shift an entire track forward or backward. Currently, our offset is zero. Similarly, you are given the opportunity to quantize each individual pitch. Between the track name and offset, select Quantize.

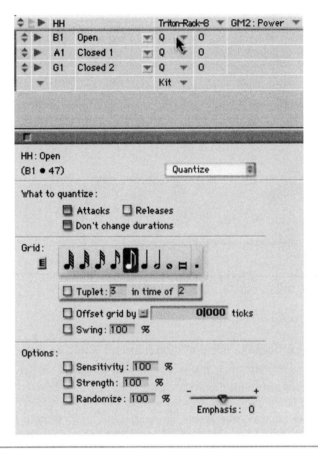

FIGURE 8.14 Quantize Individual Pitches in the Drum Editor

When you do so, the quantize window appears at the bottom left of the drum editor. Here, you can assign your favorite quantize settings: Swing percentage, Strength, and so on. In this case, the open hi-hat is being quantized to a straight eighth-note grid. You can also insert Groove Quantizing and Humanizing.

8.4 Notation Editor

If you prefer looking at written music, the Notation Editor may be the most comfortable for you. It is structured similarly to the Graphic Editor, but the piano roll portion is replaced with a music staff. Again, velocities are shown at the bottom.

Be aware that the music is notated exactly as you play it—not how you would necessarily write it out. For instance, figure 8.15 shows the bass part from "Upbeat Rock." If we were to write out the part, we would write all eighth notes (with stems up...), rather than both eighths and sixteenths:

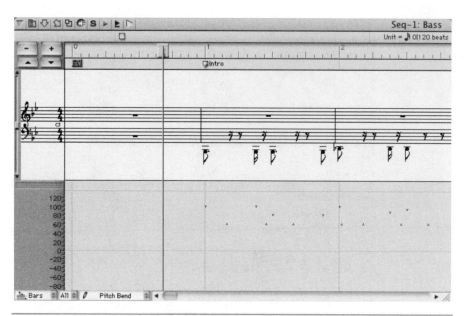

FIGURE 8.15 Notation Editor

However, if we change the notation's duration, we would be changing the actual performance! As we rarely play music exactly as it would be written out, this often changes the performance for the worse.

Often, you can to get your music to appear more accurately by setting the appropriate Unit Resolution Unit = ♪ 0|240 beats . This determines the smallest value you will see in the Notation Editor. For instance, in figure 8.15, the Unit value was set to "sixteenths." This means that if we play a staccato eighth note, as we did, it will be represented as a sixteenth note followed by a sixteenth rest. If we change the unit to eighths, Digital Performer will not draw any sixteenths, resulting in one eighth note (see figure 8.16). Usually, setting the unit to the smallest rhythmic value in the piece will produce the best results.

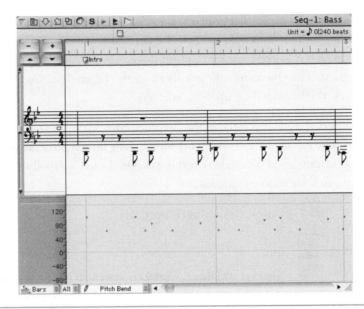

FIGURE 8.16 Notation Editor. Unit is set to eighths, producing more accurate notation.

8.5 Quickscribe Editor

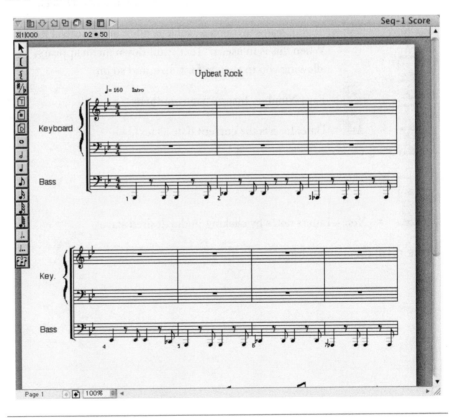

FIGURE 8.17 Quickscribe Editor

The Quickscribe Editor is used primarily for printing out parts and scores, but be careful—changing durations and pitches will again change your performance as well. Here, we have a condensed score for "Upbeat Rock," consisting of only the bass and keyboard parts. The Quickscribe Editor also uses the Expand button ⬜, allowing you to select which tracks show up in the editor.

Since we inserted the key of B-flat in the Conductor track, the score appears in the correct key. The Editor also did some work for us, using the tempo of the piece as the metronome marking, and the markers' text boxes. On the left is a toolbar that allows you to perform basic editing functions.

= Arrow. Selects and moves data.

= Bracket and Brace. Connects staves. In our project, all staves are connected with a bracket, and the two keyboard staves are connected with a brace.

= Note Speller. Changes notes to their equivalent enharmonic. For instance, if the bass part in measure 2 had shown up as C-sharps, we could use this to convert them to D-flats.

= Text. Creates text boxes, such as titles and rehearsal letters. When this is in use, a "Text" pull-down menu appears, allowing you to change font, size, and so on.

= Page Number. Inserts page numbers.

= Date. Inserts the current date as text.

= Notes. Enters notes by clicking in the desired staves.

FIGURE 8.18 Quickscribe Tools

The Quickscribe mini-menu is full of useful tools and options you should explore.

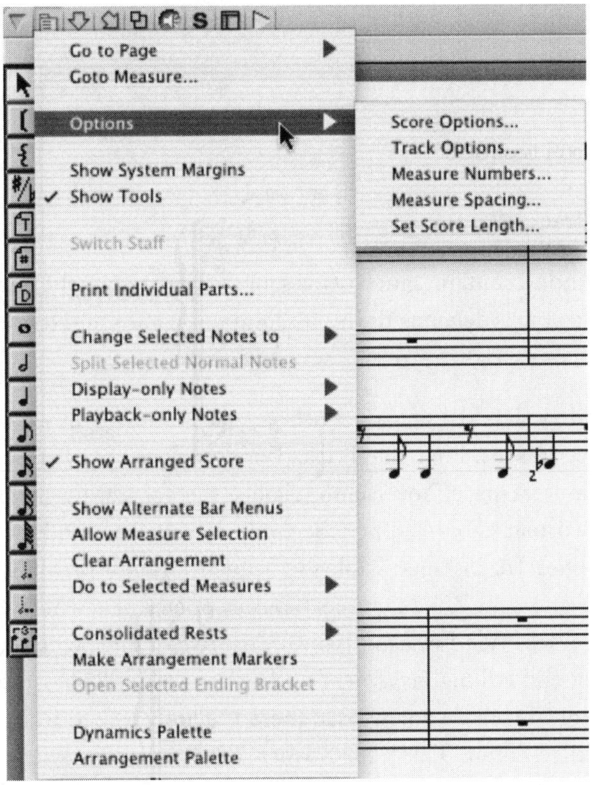

FIGURE 8.19 Quickscribe Menu

The Score and Track Options are particularly useful, giving you preferences for spacing, track names, markers, and more. There is a Transposition option in the Track Options, which is particularly useful when dealing with transposed instruments, such as saxophones. Since it is recommended that you start your music in the second measure of the sequence, you may wish to hide measure zero. To do this, choose "Allow Measure Selection," select measure zero, and choose "Do to Selected Measures → Hide."

At the bottom of the mini-menu is a Dynamics palette, which allows you to add dynamic markings and crescendos. The Arrangement palette allows you to add repeat signs, codas, and so on.

8.6 Tracks Window

Digital Performer actually has two windows that you can use to view many tracks, giving you a large-scale view of your work. The first is the Sequence Editor, and the second is the Tracks Window.

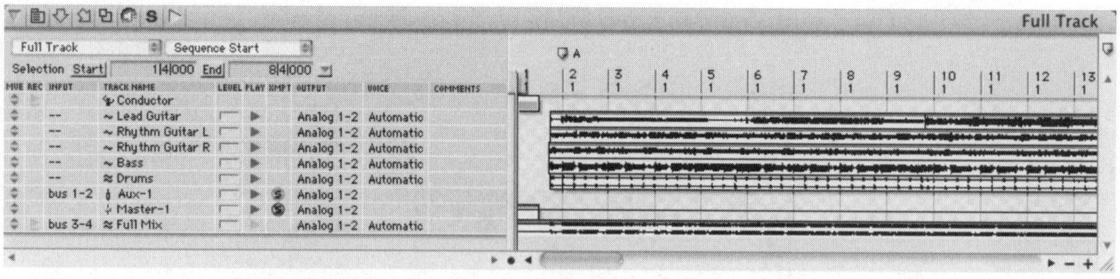

FIGURE 8.20 Tracks Window

The Tracks Window contains much of the same information as the Sequence Editor. On the left are columns detailing the inputs, outputs, names, and related information for each track. On the right are overviews of the tracks.

So, which window should you use? I believe you should begin with the Sequence Editor, for three reasons. First, the Tracks Window does not offer as many ways to customize your workspace. You cannot change the vertical height of tracks, hide tracks, or set custom zoom settings. Second, the Tracks Window has far fewer editing capabilities. For instance, while the Sequence Editor provides a Pitch Ruler for MIDI editing, Tracks Window users typically open a new window to edit MIDI tracks. In fact, Tracks Window users typically use two or three windows to complete basic recording and editing tasks, while all of the tasks can be completed in the Sequence Editor. If you are a new user, there is simply less to learn by beginning with the Sequence Editor. Third, the Sequence Editor more closely resembles the feel of other programs, such as Pro Tools and Logic. If you already know another program, or feel you may need to switch back and forth for some reason, you will feel most natural in the Sequence Editor.

That being said, many users find it easier to set and troubleshoot inputs and outputs from the Tracks Window. Since each track is short vertically, many tracks are visible in one screen. Unlike the Sequence Editor, each track's input and output is visible from this "minimized" setup.

Digital Performer provides a wide range of editing windows to give you total control of your work. They are designed to support a wide range of working methods, incorporating graphics, notation, data lists, and more. Simultaneously, they share a range of similar features, making them easy to learn and use. While you do not need to master them all, a general understanding of each is recommended, as each window is preferrable in different contexts.

RECORDING AUDIO

9.1 Analog and Digital Audio

Unlike MIDI, audio is the actual sound that you hear. Audio can be transmitted from one device to another in two basic formats: analog and digital. Both represent the actual audio waveform. Analog technologies transfer this information via an electronic pulse that travels over a wire. A lot of great musicians, over the years—such as the Beatles—recorded in an entirely analog environment. The most common complaint with an analog transfer is that the audio signal can degrade. The electronic pulse traveling over the wire will be slightly different at the destination than at the source. As a result, after multiple transfers, imperfections can arise.

Digital audio converts the audio waveform into computer data—a sequence of 1s and 0s, rather than an electronic pulse. When digital audio transfers from one device to another, it is no different than transferring computer files from one hard drive to another. All the 1s and 0s are simply sent from machine to machine. The 1s and 0s are exactly the same at the destination as they were at the source, meaning no degradation occurs. The traditional complaint about digital was that it sounded cold, or too bright. But modern technologies, such as Digital Performer, have largely overcome such perceived deficiencies. Most studios today prefer to use as much digital equipment as possible.

9.2 Sample Rate and Format

Before we begin recording, we must understand the fundamentals of how digital audio is structured and how it interacts with Digital Performer. The first aspect is sample rate and format.

SAMPLE RATE refers to how frequently an analog signal is sampled when being converted to digital audio. The sample rate is most commonly expressed in kilohertz (kHz), which is a measure of cycles per second (cps). (Digital Performer uses both standards.) A sample rate of 44.1 kHz (44,100 cps) is the standard sampling rate for CDs. Higher rates, such as 48 kHz and 96 kHz, can be used in other digital formats.

SAMPLE FORMAT (also called "bit depth") is the amount of information in each individual sample. A 16-bit format is standard for CDs, though 24-bit is common in other digital formats.

The sample rate and format are the building blocks of digital audio. Literally, they determine how much information is encoded into the files and how that information is structured. To use them effectively, there are three concepts that should concern you.

First, high sample rates and formats result in higher quality sound. Think of the sampling rate and format as the "resolution" of the music. When the resolution of a picture is higher, the picture is crisper and more accurate to the original image. The same is true in music. It is ideal to work in the highest sample rate and format your studio equipment (and client's desired product) will allow.

Second, be aware that a higher sample rate and format means more information in each file, which translates into larger files. If you record at 96 kHz, 24-bit, your hard drive will fill up roughly twice as fast as if you record at 44.1 kHz, 16-bit. Ideally your musical goals should ultimately drive your decisions, rather than your hard drive space, but if space is an issue, be conscious of your situation.

Third, all the devices and audio files you are using need to be set to the same sample rate and format. This includes, but is not limited to, the audio files on your hard drive, your audio interface, and your digital mixing board. Let's say your audio files were recorded at 44.1 kHz. If your audio hardware interprets them at 48 kHz, the audio will sound incorrectly.

The sample rate and format of the audio files is determined by the rate and format of your audio interface at the time of recording. This information can be controlled from within Digital Performer by using its Audio drawer, opened by clicking on the triangle ◤ in the upper right-hand corner of the Control Panel. In figure 9.1, you can see that the rate and format of the audio interface are set to 44.1 kHz and 16-bit. These settings will govern all the audio files created during recording.

So, your first concern is that these settings are the same as they were when you created your audio files. Changing your hardware settings will change your audio interface, but *not the audio files already created*.

FIGURE 9.1 Audio Drawer. Sample Rate and Format set to 44.1 kHz and 16 Bit.

If your audio files were recorded in a previous session, you can find out their sample rate in the Soundbites window. The Soundbites window can be opened from the Windows menu (shortcut: Shift-b).

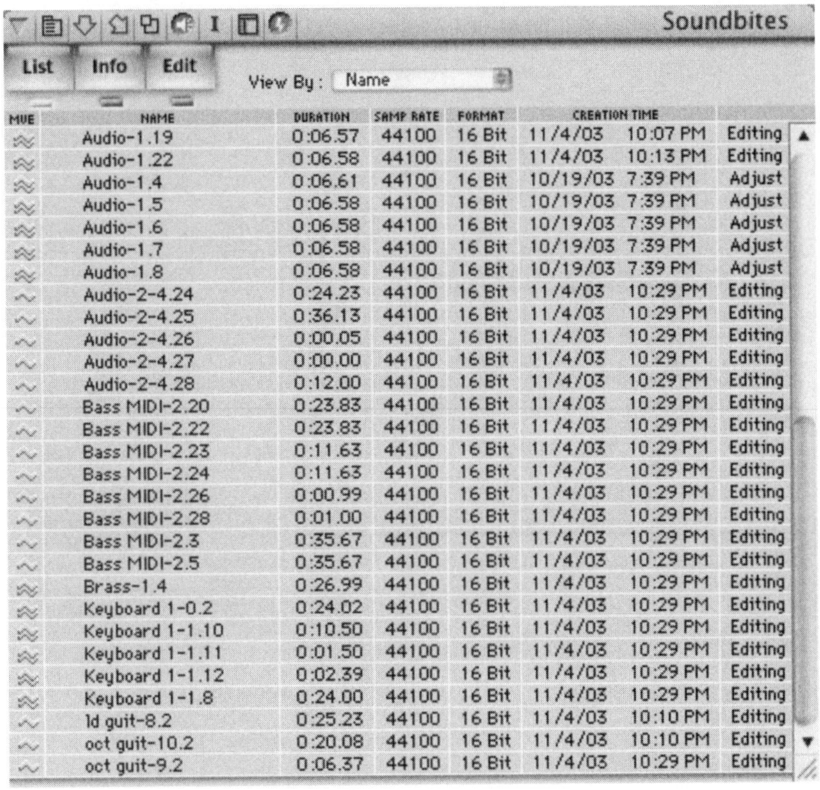

MUE	NAME	DURATION	SAMP RATE	FORMAT	CREATION TIME	
≈	Audio-1.19	0:06.57	44100	16 Bit	11/4/03 10:07 PM	Editing
≈	Audio-1.22	0:06.58	44100	16 Bit	11/4/03 10:13 PM	Editing
≈	Audio-1.4	0:06.61	44100	16 Bit	10/19/03 7:39 PM	Adjust
≈	Audio-1.5	0:06.58	44100	16 Bit	10/19/03 7:39 PM	Adjust
≈	Audio-1.6	0:06.58	44100	16 Bit	10/19/03 7:39 PM	Adjust
≈	Audio-1.7	0:06.58	44100	16 Bit	10/19/03 7:39 PM	Adjust
≈	Audio-1.8	0:06.58	44100	16 Bit	10/19/03 7:39 PM	Adjust
~	Audio-2-4.24	0:24.23	44100	16 Bit	11/4/03 10:29 PM	Editing
~	Audio-2-4.25	0:36.13	44100	16 Bit	11/4/03 10:29 PM	Editing
~	Audio-2-4.26	0:00.05	44100	16 Bit	11/4/03 10:29 PM	Editing
~	Audio-2-4.27	0:00.00	44100	16 Bit	11/4/03 10:29 PM	Editing
~	Audio-2-4.28	0:12.00	44100	16 Bit	11/4/03 10:29 PM	Editing
~	Bass MIDI-2.20	0:23.83	44100	16 Bit	11/4/03 10:29 PM	Editing
~	Bass MIDI-2.22	0:23.83	44100	16 Bit	11/4/03 10:29 PM	Editing
~	Bass MIDI-2.23	0:11.63	44100	16 Bit	11/4/03 10:29 PM	Editing
~	Bass MIDI-2.24	0:11.63	44100	16 Bit	11/4/03 10:29 PM	Editing
~	Bass MIDI-2.26	0:00.99	44100	16 Bit	11/4/03 10:29 PM	Editing
~	Bass MIDI-2.28	0:01.00	44100	16 Bit	11/4/03 10:29 PM	Editing
~	Bass MIDI-2.3	0:35.67	44100	16 Bit	11/4/03 10:29 PM	Editing
~	Bass MIDI-2.5	0:35.67	44100	16 Bit	11/4/03 10:29 PM	Editing
≈	Brass-1.4	0:26.99	44100	16 Bit	11/4/03 10:29 PM	Editing
≈	Keyboard 1-0.2	0:24.02	44100	16 Bit	11/4/03 10:29 PM	Editing
≈	Keyboard 1-1.10	0:10.50	44100	16 Bit	11/4/03 10:29 PM	Editing
≈	Keyboard 1-1.11	0:01.50	44100	16 Bit	11/4/03 10:29 PM	Editing
≈	Keyboard 1-1.12	0:02.39	44100	16 Bit	11/4/03 10:29 PM	Editing
≈	Keyboard 1-1.8	0:24.00	44100	16 Bit	11/4/03 10:29 PM	Editing
~	ld guit-8.2	0:25.23	44100	16 Bit	11/4/03 10:10 PM	Editing
~	oct guit-10.2	0:20.08	44100	16 Bit	11/4/03 10:10 PM	Editing
~	oct guit-9.2	0:06.37	44100	16 Bit	11/4/03 10:29 PM	Editing

FIGURE 9.2 Soundbites Window. Shows previously recorded audio and its sample rate and format.

The Soundbites window lists all of the audio files you have recorded or imported into your sequence. As this example shows, all of the audio files in "Upbeat Rock" were recorded at 44,100 cps (44.1 kHz) and 16-bit. Since this is the same as our hardware settings, we are good to go. If you wish to change the format or sampling rate of an audio file, you can do so in the Soundbites window. Highlight the name of the file you wish to change, and select "Convert Sample Rate" or "Convert Sample Format" from the Soundbites mini-menu.

WARNING: If there are discrepancies between your audio files and your hardware, lots of red lights go off from Digital Performer. Here, you can see that Digital Performer has placed red Xs on the audio files in the Soundbites window. This means that while the audio files are set at 44,100/16-bit, the hardware is set at something else. Likewise, if there is a problem, the Sample Rate field in the Audio Side Panel will flash red. So, be sure your audio files and hardware devices have the same sample rate and format.

MUE	NAME	DURATION	SAMP RATE	FORMAT	CREATION TIME	
✕	Audio-1.19	0:06.57	44100	16 Bit	11/4/03 10:07 PM	Editing
✕	Audio-1.22	0:06.58	44100	16 Bit	11/4/03 10:13 PM	Editing
✕	Audio-1.4	0:06.61	44100	16 Bit	10/19/03 7:39 PM	Adjust
✕	Audio-1.5	0:06.58	44100	16 Bit	10/19/03 7:39 PM	Adjust
✕	Audio-1.6	0:06.58	44100	16 Bit	10/19/03 7:39 PM	Adjust
✕	Audio-1.7	0:06.58	44100	16 Bit	10/19/03 7:39 PM	Adjust
✕	Audio-1.8	0:06.58	44100	16 Bit	10/19/03 7:39 PM	Adjust
✕	Audio-2-4.24	0:24.23	44100	16 Bit	11/4/03 10:29 PM	Editing
✕	Audio-2-4.25	0:36.13	44100	16 Bit	11/4/03 10:29 PM	Editing
✕	Audio-2-4.26	0:00.05	44100	16 Bit	11/4/03 10:29 PM	Editing
✕	Audio-2-4.27	0:00.00	44100	16 Bit	11/4/03 10:29 PM	Editing
✕	Audio-2-4.28	0:12.00	44100	16 Bit	11/4/03 10:29 PM	Editing
✕	Bass MIDI-2.20	0:23.83	44100	16 Bit	11/4/03 10:29 PM	Editing
✕	Bass MIDI-2.22	0:23.83	44100	16 Bit	11/4/03 10:29 PM	Editing
✕	Bass MIDI-2.23	0:11.63	44100	16 Bit	11/4/03 10:29 PM	Editing
✕	Bass MIDI-2.24	0:11.63	44100	16 Bit	11/4/03 10:29 PM	Editing
✕	Bass MIDI-2.26	0:00.99	44100	16 Bit	11/4/03 10:29 PM	Editing
✕	Bass MIDI-2.28	0:01.00	44100	16 Bit	11/4/03 10:29 PM	Editing
✕	Bass MIDI-2.3	0:35.67	44100	16 Bit	11/4/03 10:29 PM	Editing
✕	Bass MIDI-2.5	0:35.67	44100	16 Bit	11/4/03 10:29 PM	Editing
✕	Brass-1.4	0:26.99	44100	16 Bit	11/4/03 10:29 PM	Editing
✕	Keyboard 1-0.2	0:24.02	44100	16 Bit	11/4/03 10:29 PM	Editing
✕	Keyboard 1-1.10	0:10.50	44100	16 Bit	11/4/03 10:29 PM	Editing
✕	Keyboard 1-1.11	0:01.50	44100	16 Bit	11/4/03 10:29 PM	Editing
✕	Keyboard 1-1.12	0:02.39	44100	16 Bit	11/4/03 10:29 PM	Editing
✕	Keyboard 1-1.8	0:24.00	44100	16 Bit	11/4/03 10:29 PM	Editing
✕	ld guit-8.2	0:25.23	44100	16 Bit	11/4/03 10:10 PM	Editing
✕	oct guit-10.2	0:20.08	44100	16 Bit	11/4/03 10:10 PM	Editing
✕	oct guit-9.2	0:06.37	44100	16 Bit	11/4/03 10:29 PM	Editing

FIGURE 9.3 Format Incompatibilities Indicated Between Audio Files and Audio Interface

9.3 Digital Word Clock

You may wonder, with precision such as 44,100 cycles per second, how does your audio hardware know *exactly* how long a second is?

Digital audio gear requires some kind of timing reference in order to accurately play back audio. As a result, every piece of digital gear has an internal timing mechanism. If you are only using one digital audio device (such as your audio interface), you should set its word clock to "Internal." This can be done in the Audio side panel, as shown here. "Internal" means that it is not receiving word-clock information from another device.

FIGURE 9.4 Digital Word Clock

When you are using more than one digital audio device (such as an audio interface and a digital mixing board), you cannot set both devices to their internal clocks. In doing so, both devices would use their own clocks for timing and not be in sync with one another. You would get pops and clicks, inferior stereo imaging, and a loss of accuracy in high frequencies.

To avoid this, you must designate one device to be the "master clock" and the other devices to be the "slave clocks." The master clock will be set to "Internal," while the other devices will use it for their timing reference.

For instance, let's say that you are using an audio interface such as the MOTU 828 and a digital mixing board such as the Yamaha 02R, connected to each other with ADAT cables. In this scenario, either the 828 or the 02R could be the master. If the 828 is the master, choose "Internal" in Digital Performer. Then, go to the 02R and tell it to look over its ADAT connection for the word clock.

Likewise, you could make the 02R the master by setting its word clock to "Internal." In this scenario, you would need to slave the 828 by selecting ADAT in Digital Performer.

How to set up the sync in your studio will depend on your specific equipment. Just remember, if you have more than one digital audio device, one device needs to provide the "master" clock, and all other devices need to watch this clock for their sync.

9.4 Buffer Size

To listen to digital audio in your Digital Performer project, the audio must leave your computer and then be converted into an analog signal. When you are recording, the original signal must be converted to digital audio, recorded onto your computer, and then converted back to an analog signal, so that you can monitor it. Today's equipment computes this transfer nearly instantaneously. However, a very subtle delay can occur. The delay is referred to as *latency*.

In Digital Performer, latency is a monitoring issue only. Your audio will always be recorded in time. When recording, you should still strive for as little latency as possible. Quite often, a player is overdubbing along with tracks already recorded, for which monitoring latency may be an issue. For instance, in "Upbeat Rock," we used a virtual instrument to perform the bass part. While the guitarist is playing his part, he may be listening to this bass part, adjusting his performance to be in time with the bass. If you have latency on your bass track, this will compromise the performance of the guitarist. On the other hand, if you are mixing your final track, you would not care if there was a slight delay. Each track would be uniformly late—sounding normal to you and the DAT player or other device to which you are recording.

How do you control latency? By raising or lowering the buffer size on your audio hardware. The *buffer size* is the amount of audio samples your computer receives and processes at once. Lowering the buffer size increases the task for your computer, resulting in lower latency. However, at lower buffer settings, your computer will be less capable of processing audio plug-ins, such as reverb. For this reason, it is typically recommended to record with a low buffer size, such as 128, and play back at a higher buffer size, such as 1024. To change your buffer, click on the Hardware button in the Audio drawer.

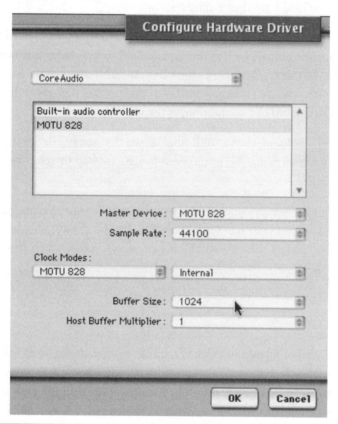

FIGURE 9.5 Changing the Buffer Size

In the Configure Hardware Driver window, you can set the Buffer Size. Here, it is being set to 1024. You can also use this window to set the Master Device, Sample Rate, and Word Clock. It is recommended to leave the Host Buffer Multiplier at 1. There are rare circumstances in which you would want to change this setting, and they are covered in the *Digital Performer User Guide*.

9.5 File Management

When recording in Digital Performer, you are creating digital audio files. These audio files exist independently of the sequence file. This means that in addition to your sequence file, you will have audio files located somewhere on your hard drive. To avoid personal agony and angry clients, keep track of your information by *always keeping your audio files folder in the same folder as your sequence file.*

FIGURE 9.6 File Structure

In figure 9.6, you can see there is a folder called "Upbeat Rock Project." Located inside this folder is a Digital Performer Sequence file, "Upbeat Rock." In addition, there is a folder called "Audio Files." Inside of the Audio Files folder are all of the audio files necessary for the sequence. With this file hierarchy, all the information needed is located in the "Upbeat Rock Project" folder. If you are backing up your project to a hard drive or CD, you must include the entire "Upbeat Rock Project" folder. If you backup only the "Upbeat Rock" sequence file, all of your audio files will be missing when you restore your file.

9.6 Audio Monitor Window

Before recording any audio in Digital Performer, you should always open the Audio Monitor window (Studio–Audio Monitor or Shift-a). This window performs four tasks:

1. It lets you monitor the level at which you are recording.
2. It determines the names of recorded audio files.
3. It tells you how much hard-drive space you have available for recording.
4. It determines where recorded audio files will be placed on your hard drive.

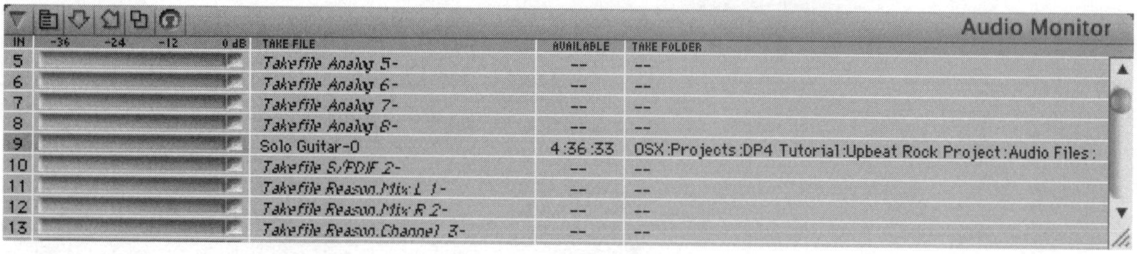

Fig. 9.7. Audio Monitor Window

In this example, you can see that there are five columns. In the middle is the "Take File" column. This tells you the name of the audio file you are about to create. This name is derived from the name of the audio track you have record-enabled—reason to name your tracks!

On the far right is the "Take Folder" column. This tells you where your audio files will be placed. In this case, they will be placed on the OSX drive, in its Projects folder, in its DP4 Tutorial folder, in its "Upbeat Rock" Project folder, and in its Audio Files folder. If you double-click on this column, it will open the folder in question.

If you wish to change where on the hard drive you are recording to, you can:

1. Click the Take File column.
2. Select "Set Take Folder" from the mini-menu.
3. Locate (click to highlight) the folder you wish to record to.
4. Select "Choose."

You can replace steps (1) and (2) by double-clicking on the "Take File" column.

The "Available" column shows you how much drive space you have available for recording. In this case, I could record for 4 hours, 36 minutes, and 33 seconds.

The "Level" column displays the level at which you are recording. Digital audio has a theoretical limit of 0 db, which you must never exceed. Likewise, it is important not to record with the level too low. This will increase the noise level, when compared to the music. At some point, you will compensate for the low level and raise the gain of the signal. When you do so, you are also raising the level of the background noise you recorded. When recording, try to get your input level somewhere between –12 db and 0 db.

On the far left is an IN (input) number—in our case, number 9. Every possible input, including the analog and digital inputs on your audio hardware, the internal busses, and outputs of software synths such as Reason, is assigned a number. How do you know which input is assigned to the input you are recording to? First, be sure that your track is record-enabled. Then, scroll down through the Audio Monitor until you find the input that is red.

9.7 Inputs and Outputs

As with MIDI tracks, we must properly set the inputs and outputs of the audio tracks. Obviously, these will vary greatly, depending on the setup of your studio.

The "output" settings determine where the audio signal is sent during playback. If you are using a high-end audio interface in addition to a large mixing board, you will have many options here. You could choose between different analog and digital outputs, depending upon where you wished the signal to come up on the mixing board. If you are using a smaller interface or internal computer speakers, you will have fewer choices.

The input setting determines what signal is recorded.

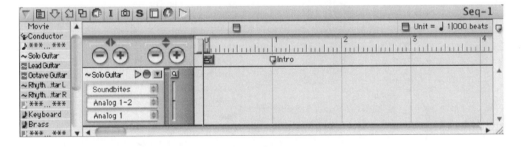

FIGURE 9.8 Setting Audio Inputs and Outputs

In this example, the audio input is set to Analog 1. This refers to Analog 1 of your audio interface, which in the case of the MOTU 828 is a mic preamp. This means we are recording the signal from a microphone that is connected to our Mic Input 1. This would be the case if we placed a microphone in front of our guitar amplifier.

The output is set to Analog 1–2. This routes the incoming audio to our audio interface main outputs, which presumably are connected to our amplifier and monitoring speakers.

When you select an input or output, you are actually selecting an audio bundle. An *audio bundle* is a group of inputs, outputs, or busses. For instance, it is common to group analog 1 and analog 2 together as a stereo bundle, referenced as "Analog 1–2."

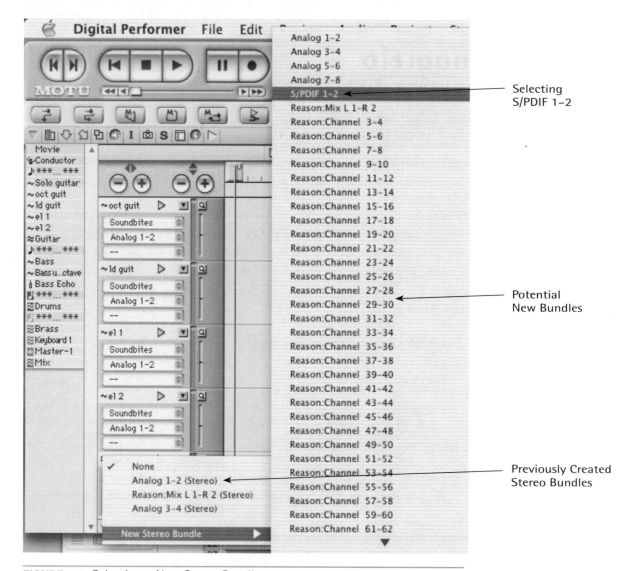

FIGURE 9.9 Selecting a New Stereo Bundle

To create a new bundle, click on your input or output, drag down to "New Bundle >," and select from the full list. Previously defined bundles will appear on a short list when clicking on your input or output.

This organization provides several benefits. For instance, you will not need to repeatedly sift through all of your potential settings. If you are setting multiple outputs to "Analog 1–2," you must select it from the full list only once, after which you can use the short list.

In addition, these bundles can be renamed and manipulated with the Audio Bundles window (shortcut: Shift-u).

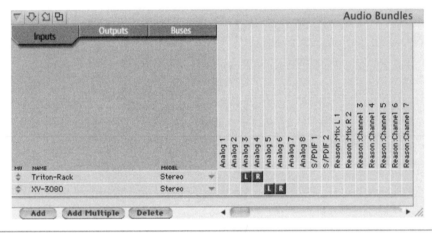

FIGURE 9.10 Audio Bundles Window

In figure 9.10, the "Inputs" tab is selected in the upper left. This means Analog 1 refers to "Analog 1 In" on our audio interface, and so on. You can rename a bundle by option or double-clicking on the bundle name. Notice I've named the bundle assigned to Analog 3–4 "Triton-Rack." This is because we previously connected our Triton-Rack audio output to Analog 3–4 In of our audio interface. Similarly, we renamed Analog 5–6 to "XV-3080." In addition, we could rename Analog 1–2 Out to "Main Out," via the Outputs tab.

After doing so, our Aux track assignments will be named more logically.

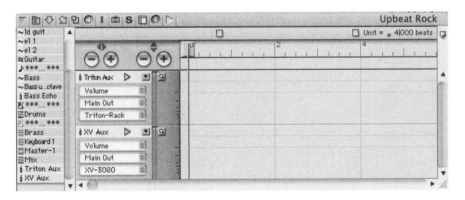

FIGURE 9.11 Aux Tracks. Audio Inputs and Outputs renamed via the Audio Bundles window.

Audio bundles save you time when rewiring your studio. For instance, if you purchase a digital amplifier and use your S/PDIF connection as your main output, then you would need to switch every output for your audio, aux, and instrument tracks. Rather than reassigning all of these outputs, you could simply reassign the Main Out audio bundle.

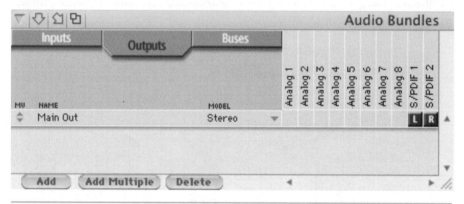

FIGURE 9.12 Main Out Audio Bundle Reassigned

9.8 Ready to Record

At this point, we are ready to record. The steps to get here include:

1. Create and name an audio track.
2. Set the appropriate inputs and outputs.
3. Record-enable the audio track.
4. Verify the sample rate and format.
5. Verify that word clock is set appropriately.
6. Lower the buffer setting.
7. Open the Audio Monitor and check the Take Folder.
8. Click Record, monitoring levels in the Audio Monitor.

After recording guitar, "Upbeat Rock" is shaping up nicely.

TRACK 8

P05
UPBEAT
GUITAR

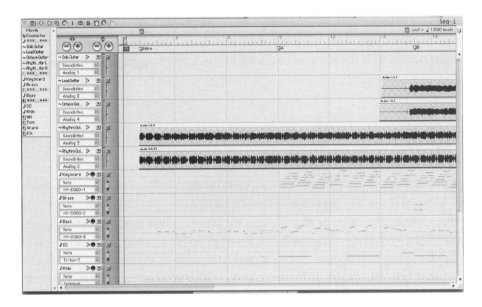

FIGURE 9.13 "Upbeat Rock"

9.9 Other Audio Sources

The audio you have in your sequence will typically arrive via one of three ways: recording live performances, loading audio files from a hard drive or CD, or converting tracks from MIDI to audio.

Importing audio from a disk is relatively painless. As with any computer file, an audio file can be in various formats. Common audio formats include AIFF, SDII, WAV, and MP3. To be used in a Digital Performer sequence, an audio file must be in Sound Designer II (SDII) format, and stereo files must be "split SDII," meaning they are actually two mono files—one for the left channel and one for the right channel.

In the title bar of the Sequence Editor is a lightning bolt 🔊 icon, referring to Automatic Conversion. Be sure this is on. It used to be that Digital Performer would ask your permission before converting audio files to the necessary format and locating them in your Audio Files folder. Now, with the Automatic Conversion feature activated, Digital Performer does this for you, which can be a time-saver. At this point, you're ready to import audio files into your Digital Performer project.

After checking to make sure Automatic Conversion is on, importing audio files is simply a matter of dragging the audio file icon onto an appropriate track in the

Sequence Editor. If you are importing a stereo file, locate it in your finder, and then drag its icon onto a stereo track in Digital Performer. Alternatively, you can use the Insert button **I** in the Sequence Editor's title bar, but dragging the icon is almost always easier.

9.10 Audio Voices

An *audio voice* is a channel on which Digital Performer can play audio. During playback, you will need sufficient audio voices to hear all of your tracks. The number of voices available will depend on your system and how you choose to allocate the voices that are available to you. If you have allocated four mono voices and then ask Digital Performer to play back five mono audio files, one of the audio files will not play. If you have many audio tracks and some of them are not playing at all, this is quite likely your problem. In our case, we currently need only five mono-audio voices, which should be no problem at all.

To check your audio voice allocation, click on the settings button **Settings...** in the Audio side panel.

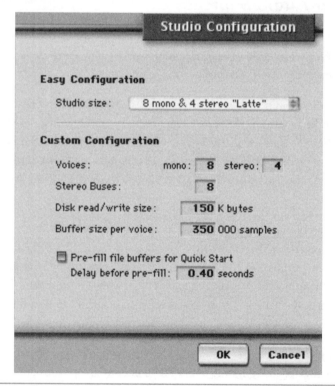

FIGURE 9.14 Studio Configuration. Used to check audio voice allocation.

Currently, we have eight mono and four stereo voices allocated. This will be plenty for our "Upbeat Rock" tune. Why not always set it to five million voices? Because each potential voice requires computer processing power. Users with older systems will have to restrain themselves.

Today's digital audio workstations have awesome potential. With Digital Performer, not only can you utilize your MIDI tools, but you can also record live instrumentals when MIDI won't suffice. With these combined tools, there are hundreds and thousands of musical effects you can create, all from the comfort of your home studio.

EDITING AUDIO

When recording live audio, performers rarely give their best performance all in one take. Editing audio lets you combine different takes, change timings, and alter durations to create a composite performance.

10.1 Soundbites

In Digital Performer, a *soundbite* is a portion of an audio file. Digital Performer lists all of the soundbites in your sequence in the Soundbites window (shortcut: Shift-b). In figure 10.1, you can see that there is one original file, "Bass MIDI-2." All the other bass soundbites are derived from this file.

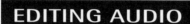

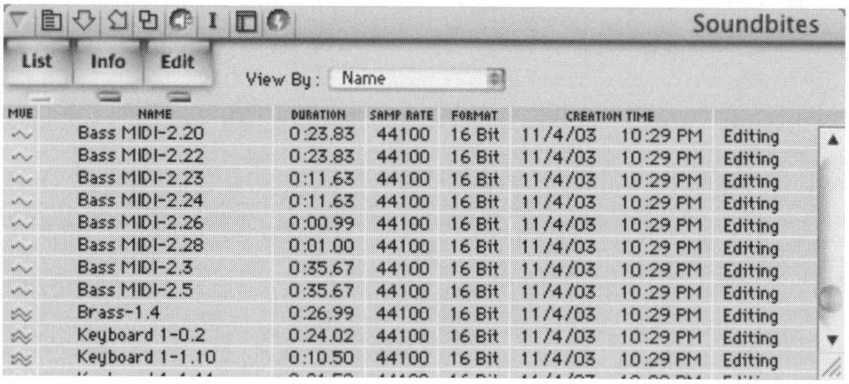

FIGURE 10.1 Soundbites Window

The Soundbites Window is arranged in columns, with each column showing different information about each soundbite, such as duration, sample rate, and format. Which columns are visible is determined by the settings in the Column Setup window, accessed from the mini-menu. In this example, the soundfile name, disk name, and so on are checked, so they will be visible in the Soundbites window. You may wish to view additional settings, such as tempo, creation time, and source.

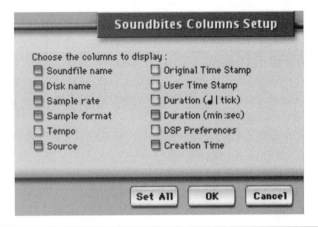

FIGURE 10.2 Soundbites Column Setup

10.2 Audio Track Cursors

As in MIDI tracks, the cursor changes shapes as you move it around an audio track. Each cursor allows you to complete different editing tasks.

ARROW

When the cursor is above the top three-quarters of a soundbite, it is shaped like an arrow. Dragging the soundbite will move it from one place to another. The grid will restrict this movement when the Edit Resolution Toggle is on.

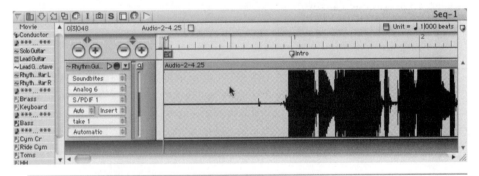

FIGURE 10.3 Arrow Cursor

CROSS–HAIR

When the cursor is positioned within the bottom quarter of a soundbite (or whenever you hold down the Control key), it is shaped as a cross-hair. You can then select the inner portions of the soundbite. In figure 10.4, the guitar part is selected from approximately 1|4|120 to 2|2|120. You are able to delete it, if you wish, without affecting anything else in the track.

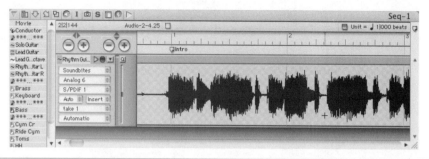

FIGURE 10.4 Crosshair Cursor

TRIMMER

When the cursor is over the edge of an audio file, whether the beginning or the end, the Trimmer cursor appears. This allows you to crop the edges of the soundbite. This is useful for deleting dead space at the beginning and the end of the soundbite.

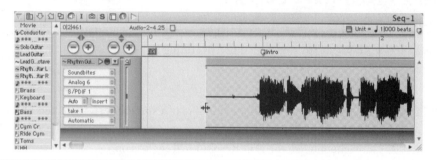

FIGURE 10.5 Trimmer Cursor

FINGER

The Finger cursor appears when the cursor is over a soundbite that has already been highlighted. For the most part, the Finger acts like the Arrow. When you drag, the soundbite will be moved, not highlighted or trimmed. *If you hold down Option, the hand will have two fingers. In this case, when you drag, the soundbite will be duplicated—a shortcut for Copy and Paste.*

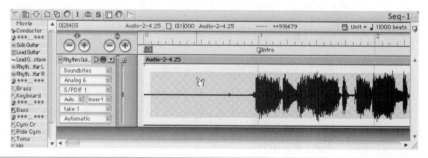

FIGURE 10.6 Finger Cursor

I-BEAM

As with MIDI tracks, you can select audio within a soundbite by using the I-Beam tool, which you can choose from the tool palette or by double-clicking your soundbite (shortcut: i). As with MIDI tracks, the I-Beam makes a time-range selection. This means you are selecting the top soundbite *and* any data that is beneath it. In figure 10.7, the I-Beam is used to select a guitar lick around measure 4.

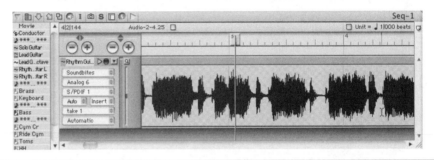

FIGURE 10.7 I-Beam Cursor

SCISSORS

As with MIDI, the Scissors tool can be used to splice audio, dividing a soundbite into two separate soundbites. In figure 10.8, the Scissors have spliced the audio just after measure 2, beat 2.

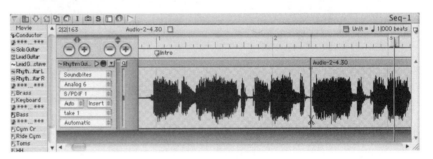

FIGURE 10.8 Scissors Cursor

In addition, you can drag on top of the soundbite with the scissors. When you do so, it splices at whatever increment the Unit value is set to. In figure 10.9, a splice is made every eighth note. This is very handy if you are working on loop-based music and want to isolate individual hits.

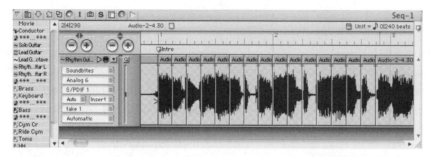

FIGURE 10.9 Eighth-Note Splices

10.3 Removing Unwanted Space

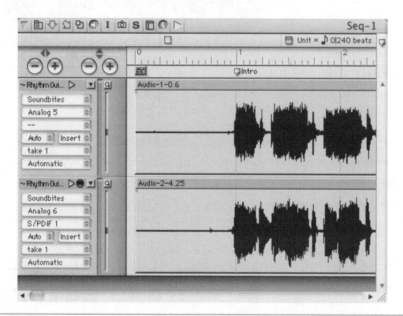

FIGURE 10.10 Unwanted Space

These cursors will help you accomplish a variety of editing tasks. First among them is deleting unwanted material, as in trimming the dead space at the beginning of audio tracks. For example, if you are recording a guitar, there is often a quiet buzz coming from the preamp, even when the guitarist is not playing. If you are recording vocals or instrumentals with a microphone, there is often miscellaneous noise, such as breathing, scuffling with the music/mic, or stray comments from the musicians. In the rhythm-guitar tracks of "Upbeat Rock," there should be empty space throughout measure 0. On the recording there was a quiet hum from the preamp, and the guitarist lightly touched the strings at certain points in this silence. Using the trimmer tool, this space at the beginning was omitted.

FIGURE 10.11 Unwanted Space Removed

Not all unwanted material will be conveniently located at the beginning or end of a soundbite. To remove material from the middle of a soundbite, first highlight it with the Cross-hair or I-Beam cursor, then hit Delete. In figure 10.12, measure 19 of a stereo drum track has been removed.

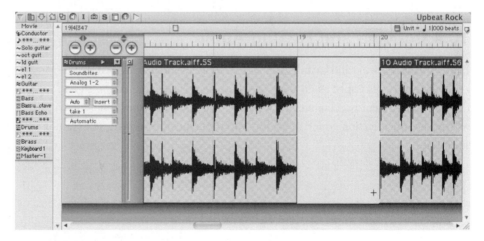

FIGURE 10.12 Deletion within a Soundbite

This leaves a large, gaping hole while everything from measure 20 onward remains where it was before the edit. Sometimes, this is what you want. Other times, you may want Digital Performer to close up this hole for you by sliding the soundbite from measure 20 back to measure 19. This is done with an editing function called Snip, rather than hitting Delete.

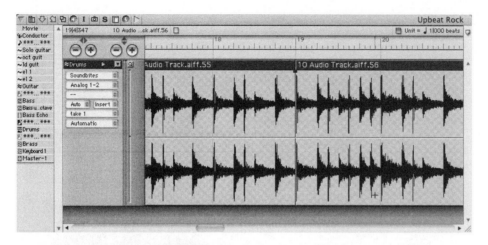

FIGURE 10.13 Deletion Closed Up

In figure 10.13, measure 19 was highlighted with the cross-hair cursor. Then, by choosing Edit–Snip, it deleted measure 19 and moved the material that had previously been at measure 20 back to measure 19, thus filling in the gap. But be careful, when choosing an editing command, such as Snip. If you need this drum track to line up with other tracks later on in the sequence, it will now be a measure early.

Using Snip can be very helpful when working with drum music or creating "cutdowns" (when a track is edited down to a much shorter version).

10.4 Copying and Pasting Audio

In many ways, copying and pasting audio is like copying and pasting MIDI. The same keyboard shortcuts apply, as do the Copy, Cut, and Paste commands. In addition, the Repeat and Set Loop commands work with audio. The major difference is that with audio, the selection you wish to copy and paste must be its own, self-contained soundbite.

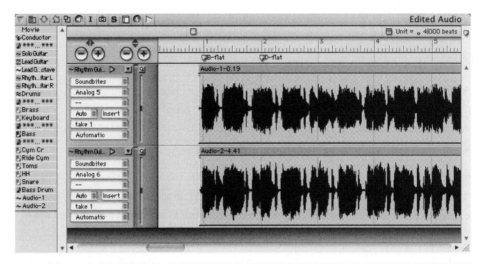

FIGURE 10.14 Rhythm Guitar as One Soundbite

In the rhythm-guitar track to "Upbeat Rock," the first measure is on a B-flat chord, followed by a D-flat chord. Let's say we wish to copy and paste the measure of D-flat. First, we must isolate the D-flat portion as its own soundbite. Highlight the desired portion with the cross-hair or I-Beam tool, and then choose Edit–Split (shortcut: Command-y).

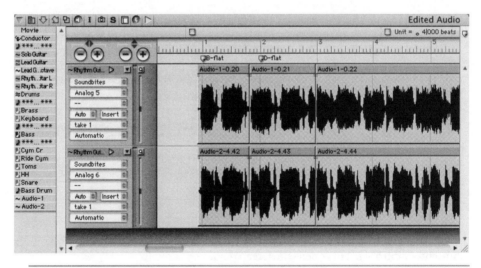

FIGURE 10.15 Isolating an Audio Region as a New Soundbite. Choose Edit–Split or use the Scissors tool.

This task could also be accomplished by using the Scissors at the start and end points of the selected region. Now that the D-flat section is isolated, we can copy and paste it as we like.

10.5 Fades

FADE–INS AND FADE–OUTS

A "fade" is a continuous volume change. *Fading in* means "getting louder," and *fading out* means "getting softer." A graph of these volume changes forms a line or curve, the exact shape of which will vary, depending on how gradual and symmetric the volume changes will be.

Each soundbite can have a fade-in at the beginning and a fade-out at the end. A fade will accomplish one of two things for you. First, you can use fades to create musical effects, essentially adding a crescendo to your audio track. Second, you can use fades to clean up edits, removing pops or other unwanted sounds.

In the lead guitar part from "Upbeat Rock," we trimmed off the dead space before the guitars came in. When trimming off empty space at the beginning and end of a soundbite, it is a good idea to leave a small amount of extra space so that you can place a quick fade in or out. If you listen closely, there is a slight pop when the soundbite begins. To avoid this, we can place a short fade at the beginning of the soundbite. This causes the audio to come in gradually, removing the pop.

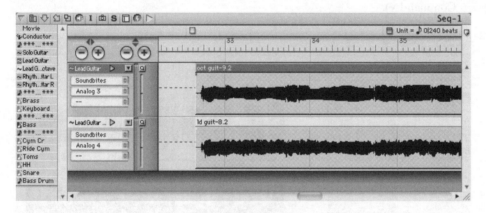

FIGURE 10.16 Guitar Parts, Ready for Fades

To add a fade, select the beginning of the soundbite, and choose Audio–Fade (shortcut: Control-f). This opens the Create Fades window.

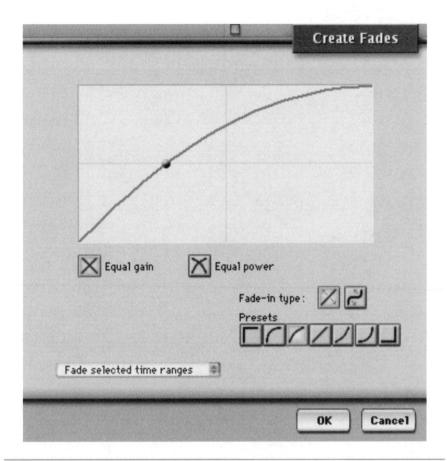

FIGURE 10.17 Create Fades Window

When the beginning of the soundbite is selected, Digital Performer assumes you want a fade-in. You can choose a fade-in type: either one-point or two-point. In figure 10.17, a one-point curve is selected with a slight arc shape. Once the shape has been selected, you can adjust the shape by dragging a point.

If you desire an S-shaped curve, select a two-point fade type, and then adjust the points as you desire.

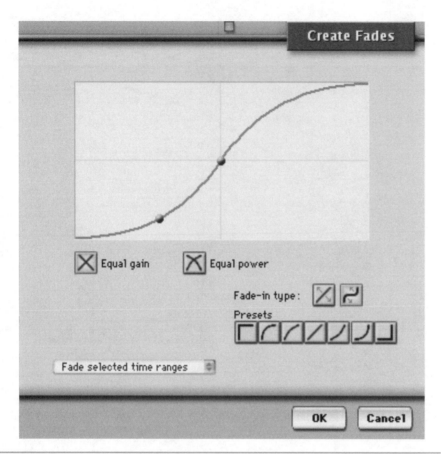

FIGURE 10.18 Two-Point Curve

Once you are happy with the fade, click OK. In figure 10.19, the fade has been created and the pop removed.

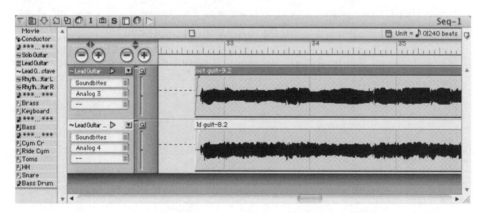

FIGURE 10.19 Soundbites with Fade-in

Fade-outs work the same as fade-ins, but apply to the end of the soundbite. Highlight the end of the soundbite, choose Audio–Fade, select your fade shape, and click OK. Here, a fade-out has been created over bars 48–50.

P06
FADE IN
AND OUT

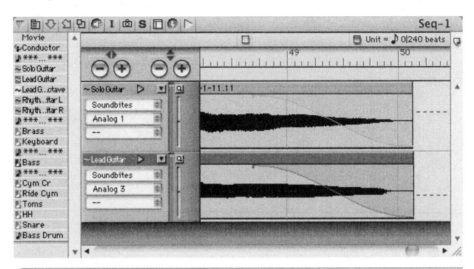

FIGURE 10.20 Fade-out

CROSSFADES

A *crossfade* combines a fade-in and a fade-out, producing a cross shape. It is used when two soundbites overlap.

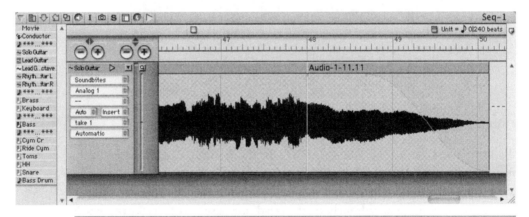

FIGURE 10.21 Guitar Track without Crossfade

Figure 10.21 shows a section of the solo guitar track from "Upbeat Rock." Note the edit at measure 48. Though this is a clean edit, another pesky pop arises. The speaker must jump from wherever it was in the first waveform, to wherever it needs to be for the second waveform. This pop can be fixed with a crossfade. Select across the edit point between the soundbites, using the cross-hair or I-Beam cursor. Where you select will determine the boundaries of the crossfade. The left boundary determines where the second soundbite will begin fading in. The right boundary determines where the first soundbite completes fading out.

After selecting the region for the crossfade, choose Audio–Fade (shortcut: Control-f), to open the Fade window. However, instead of having either a fade-in or a fade-out, you will be able to select *both* shapes. In figure 10.22, the fade-out is an S-curve, while the fade-in is a slightly raised arc. Which fade is best will depend upon the material that is being faded.

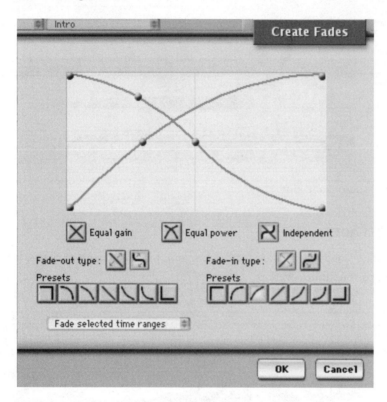

FIGURE 10.22 Designing a Crossfade

To manipulate the fade-in and fade-out individually, select the "Independent" feature. With "Equal gain" selected, the result of the crossfade will always have the same gain as the original material. This is not the case with "Equal Power," which will always place the same fade on both. If this fade is a raised-arc fade, the result will be a crossfade that raises the overall gain. If this fade is a lowered-arc fade, the result will be a crossfade that lowers the overall gain.

Figure 10.23 shows the crossfade that results from the above settings.

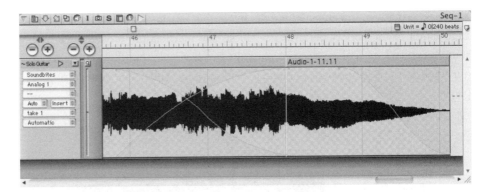

FIGURE 10.23 Audio with Crossfade over Large Area

Listen to the crossfade in figure 10.23. You can hear how the second soundbite slowly fades in. The benefit is that the awkward edit was replaced by a smooth transition. However, this crossfade is not ideal, because it no longer sounds like one guitarist playing one take. In this scenario, it would be better to create a smaller fade.

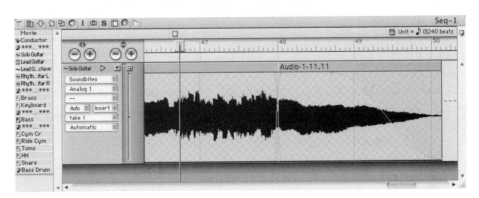

FIGURE 10.24 Smaller Crossfade

The fade in figure 10.24 still smoothes out the edit. However, now it sounds as if the guitarist played it this way.

10.6 Creating a Composite Performance

Given the ability to cut and splice and the ability to smooth overlaps and entrances, it is very easy to combine elements from imperfect takes to create one composite take. For instance, in figure 10.25, there are two takes of the same trumpet line. Unfortunately, in the first take, the performer faded out too quickly in measures 27 and 28. On the second pass, the ending was perfect, but he missed a note in measure 23 (fire that trumpet player!).

Not to worry. We can easily combine the beginning of take 1 with the end of take 2, resulting in the perfect performance. First, use the Scissors tool to slice both soundbites at a logical place. Second, place the two desirable soundbites together on one track. Last, use a crossfade to blend the splice point. Voila! The perfect trumpet player.

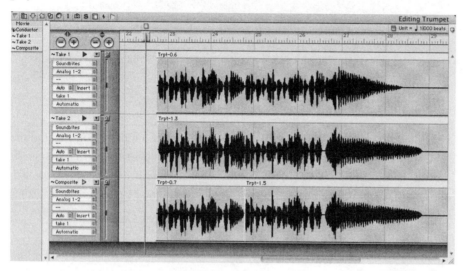

FIGURE 10.25 Creating a Composite Performance

Remember, you do not need to place each take on a separate track. You can use the "Take" feature in the Track Information Panel to place all three takes on the same track.

10.7 Non-Destructive Editing

Up until this point, all of the changes that we have made to these audio files have been non-destructive. By that I mean that all of the original audio files are still located unaltered on the hard drive, and they could be retrieved at any time. Our edits have been in the ways that Digital Performer will render these files, rather than changing the files themselves.

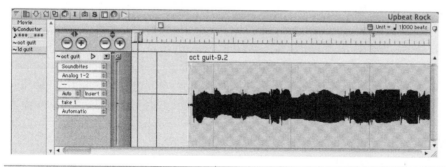

FIGURE 10.26 Soundbites

In this example, the original file was called "oct guit-9." When you trim off the beginning, you are only using a region of the audio file. Digital Performer does not create a new audio file consisting only of this region. This would use up too much hard drive space. It also does not trim off the front of the original audio, because if it did, you would not be able to undo your work. Rather, it creates a "Soundbite," in this case named "oct guit-9.2." A soundbite is a representation of the original file; "oct guit-9.2" is a region within the original audio file "oct guit-9." Each time you make an edit, Digital Performer makes a new soundbite, titling them incrementally "oct guit-9.1, oct guit-9.2, oct guit-9.3, etc."

10.8 Deleting Unused Audio

If your file contains a lot of audio, your project folder can get very large. The Soundbites window provides you the opportunity to delete audio files you are not using from your hard drive. This is a destructive edit; once you delete them, it can't be undone.

In the mini-menu, you can select the soundbites you are not using. Then, you can delete them from the same mini-menu. In addition, you may not be using all of the material in the remaining soundbites. It could be that you trimmed off 1:15 of a 2:00 soundbite. Since you are not using the 1:15, you can delete this with the Compact command, also in the mini-menu. Be sure to preserve some time around each soundbite. This extra time is needed for crossfades.

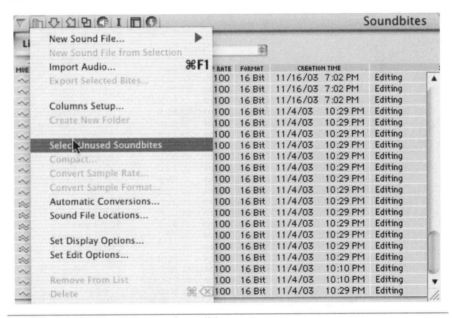

FIGURE 10.27 Select Unused Soundbites

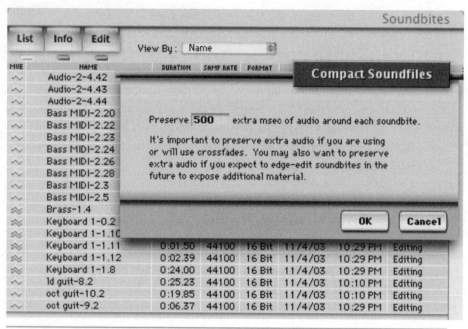

FIGURE 10.28 Compact Soundfiles

BE AWARE: These commands delete the actual audio files off your hard drive. If you are not 100 percent absolutely sure that you will not need them again, then do not execute these commands.

MIXING

Digital Performer provides an internal mixing environment that allows you to do all of your mixing on your computer. You can also work in conjunction with an external mixing board.

11.1 Mixing Board Layout

This is Digital Performer's Mixing Board, which can be opened from the Project menu (shortcut: Shift-m). These are the current Mixing Board settings for "Upbeat Rock."

FIGURE 11.1 Mixing Board for "Upbeat Rock"

As with most editing windows, the Mixing Board has an "Expand"  feature, allowing you to show and hide individual tracks.

11.2 Setting Volumes

Digital Performer's mixer looks much like a hardware mixer. Each track has its own individual volume fader. The volume is set by dragging the fader up and down, clicking the – or + buttons, or by typing a value in the field. This fader has been set to a volume level of 118.

In the case of MIDI tracks, the volume has a range of 0 to 127. This value will be sent to the sound module, synthesizer, or sampler that is designated as the output for this track. For our bass part, the output device is the XV-3080-3, so channel 3 of the XV-3080 will be set to a volume of 118.

FIGURE 11.2   Volume Fader

Each channel of a sound module or synthesizer has only one volume setting. For instance, channel 2 on the XV-3080 cannot have a volume setting of 127 and 80 simultaneously. If you have multiple MIDI tracks set to the same output channel, the different faders are irrelevant; each track will end up with the same settings. This is why I recommend that each MIDI drum track be given its own individual output.

For audio tracks, the volume range is –∞ to +6 dB. It is dangerous to push audio tracks above 0 dB. If the audio track itself was recorded near 0 dB, and the Mixing Board setting is +6 dB, the end result will be distorted.

Unlike MIDI tracks, the volume level for audio tracks can vary, even if each track has the same output. If three audio tracks are set to Analog 1–2, and the track levels are 0 dB, –2.5 dB, and –6 dB, these level changes will be reflected in the mix.

11.3 Setting Panning

Each track also has a panpot. Panning moves the sound left to right in the stereo field. You can change the pan setting by either dragging on the panpot knob ⊙, typing in the pan setting readout 64, or clicking on the arrows next to the pan readout ◁ 64 ▷.

FIGURE 11.3 Panpot

In this example, the panpot is set right up the middle, which for a MIDI track is 64. For MIDI tracks, the panning range is 0 to 127. A value of 0 is hard left, 127 is hard right, and 64 is straight up the middle. As with volume, this information will be sent to the sound module or synthesizer and applied to the appropriate output. Once again, each output will have only one setting.

For audio, the range is <63 (left 63) to 64> (right 64). A value of 0 is straight up the middle.

11.4 A Basic Mix

It is common practice to eventually convert MIDI tracks into audio so that we have entirely audio tracks in our final mix. Then we can send each track to the same output, allowing us to mix all audio tracks entirely in Digital Performer.

Here's our new Sequence Editor. Notice how each output is set to Analog 1–2.

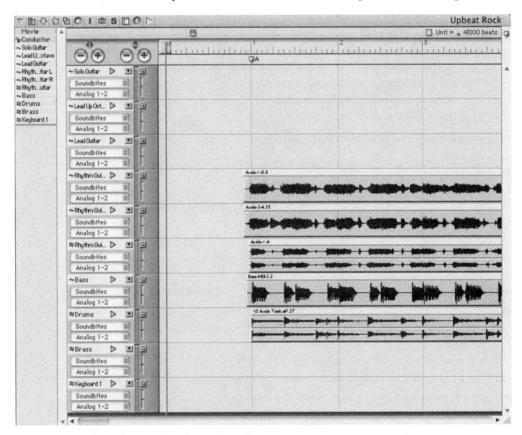

FIGURE 11.4 MIDI Tracks Converted to Audio

Next, we'll create a basic mix, starting with volume and pan settings. The volumes are set so that no one element sticks out above the others and each element can be heard. Set some basic pannings. At this point: the Rhythm Guitar L is panned left, and the Rhythm Guitar R is panned right. The other elements are panned so that there is a wide spread, but each element has its own place.

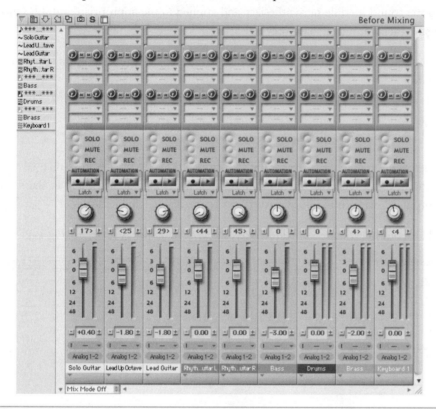

FIGURE 11.5 Basic Mix

The key to a good mix is spread and balance. It is good to have things balanced evenly left and right. Not everything should be on the right, and not everything should be on the left. Overall, as a unit, the music should be balanced in the stereo field.

With that in mind, create as wide a spread as you can. Having each element straight up the middle will result in a balanced but boring mix. Having several elements left and several elements right will result in a balanced and spread mix.

When you try to get a balanced spread, first think horizontally. Primarily, this refers to left and right placement of elements. Also think vertically. Each instrument should occupy a specific frequency range, while the combined effect of all the instruments should cover a wide range of human hearing. This is accomplished through the judicious use of EQ. Last, consider the depth. Instruments will seem farther away with reverb added. Not every element of your tune should be soaked in reverb, but some elements will require it. EQ, reverb, and many other effects are controlled in Digital Performer using effects plug-ins.

11.5 Effects

Most good mixes include the use of some effects: reverbs, EQs, delays, etc. We can add effects from the Mixing Board, which applies them in real time, during playback. The effects can be inserted in the fields at the top of each channel strip.

AUDIO INSERTS

If you click on one of the effect "insert" fields, you will see a menu of the available effects. In this case, an Echo effect has been applied to the rhythm guitar and keyboard tracks.

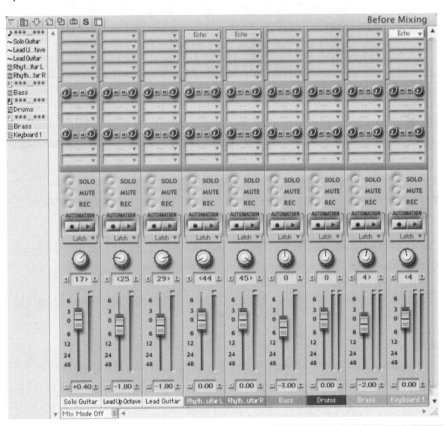

FIGURE 11.6 Echo Effect Applied to the Guitars and Keyboard

The Echo effect I used in "Upbeat Rock" is very subtle, but helps to give depth to both instruments. In the Echo plug-in window, you can set the delay times to be expressed in beats or real time (in the Tempo Lock section). In this case, it is set to beats, with an echo occurring at an eighth, quarter, and dotted-quarter note. The eighth and dotted-quarter settings are very subtle, with a gain setting of only 0.01. The quarter note is more prominent, with a gain setting of 0.10. The appropriate delay time and gain settings will depend entirely upon the source audio to which you are adding the Echo.

FIGURE 11.7 Echo Plug-in

There are two features here that are common to all effects plug-ins. The first is the Mix percentage, which controls two signals: the *input* signal and the *processed* signal. In this case, the input signal is the original rhythm-guitar track. The processed signal is an echo. The mix percentage is the ratio between these two signals. At 50%, you hear equal amounts of both. At 100%, you hear only the processed signal. At 0%, you hear only the input signal.

The second feature common to all effects is the Bypass button. This lets you quickly bypass or mute the effect, allowing you to hear the mix as it is, with no plug-in.

> To quickly bypass an effect, Option-click it on the Mixing Board. Bypassed SHORTCUT
> plug-ins appear in *italics* .

Different musical genres require different effects and settings. While I cannot give you the absolute answers for how to set up your project, we can discuss what I did with the "Upbeat Rock" tune.

After setting levels and panning, we could add various EQs to each instrument. The goal here is to give each element its own "space" by dropping unnecessary frequencies.

Here, you can see the EQ on the bass and the rhythm guitar. You may notice that more frequencies are lowered than raised. This is because raising frequencies runs the risk of distorting hot signals. If you wish to boost the upper frequencies, you could, in fact, accomplish this by either raising the high end *or* reducing the low end. But it is much safer to reduce the low end, and the end result will be the same.

In figure 11.8, the bass part has been lowered in the high end, with a touch of reduction around 200 Hz. The guitar, on the other hand, has its low frequencies cut out and a slight boost around 5,000 Hz.

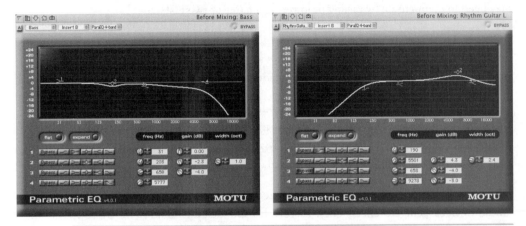

FIGURE 11.8 Setting EQ for Bass and Guitar

Figure 11.9 shows the EQs for the synth and the brass. Notice that both have their low frequencies removed. The brass has a boost around 8,000 Hz, while the keyboard is boosted around 1,500 Hz.

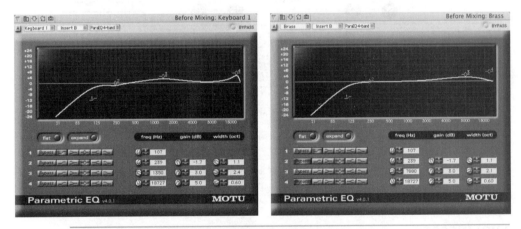

FIGURE 11.9 EQ Settings for Synth and Brass

When you look at the combined result, you notice the bass alone occupies the low end. All other instruments have the low end removed. This allows the listener to hear the bass clearly while reducing "muddiness" from other instruments. Each of the other instruments has a boost in its individual range, which helps the color of the instrument. The boost around 5,000 Hz helps the crunchiness of the guitar. The midrange boost of the keyboard gives it body, while the high-end boost gives it sparkle. The 10,000 Hz boost of the brass helps the attack and brightness.

Most importantly, EQ helps the clarity of each element while helping the mix to remain full. You may have to revisit some of your level settings, at this point. When you set EQs, you are raising and lowering the signals of particular elements, and you may need to compensate by raising or lowering a fader or two just a touch.

If you are working with MIDI tracks, you will quickly notice that the MIDI tracks do not have the same inserts available. You cannot add many traditional effects, such as reverb and EQ, to MIDI. How then, can you add reverb to your MIDI tracks?

You have three choices. First, most sound modules and synthesizers can add basic effects to the sounds they generate. While the synth is converting your MIDI performance to audio, it will add reverb etc. To do this, you will have to get to know your sound module well. Consult your manual.

Second, you could use an outboard, hardware effects module, such as a PCM80. These devices generate effects such as reverbs and delays. Somewhere in your signal flow, the audio would be sent to this device. The device would then return the processed signal.

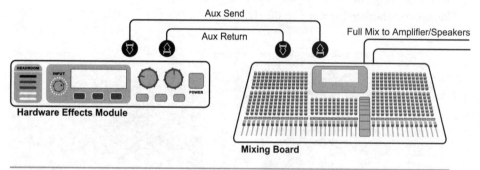

FIGURE 11.10 Mixing Board with Hardware Effects Module

Third, you could convert your MIDI tracks to audio tracks (see section 13.1). Once they are audio, you can use the built-in audio effects within Digital Performer.

MIDI INSERTS

Rather than processing the ultimate audio signal, inserts on MIDI tracks alter the MIDI data created during playback. As one example, you can add an "Echo" insert to a MIDI track. During playback, Digital Performer would echo each note by generating an additional Note On message at the appropriate interval.

There are times when the MIDI inserts will help you a great deal. You can assign quantization, transposition, and other effects. Notably, the data on the track is visually unchanged. Let's say you are inputting a transposed, orchestral score. While setting up your file, you can assign the appropriate transposition plug-ins in the

Mixing Board. When recording the parts, you can play them as written. They will show up on the track at the written pitch, allowing for easy editing. However, during playback, the insert in the Mixing Board will transpose each track to concert pitch.

11.6 Internal Bussing

A *bus* is a path to send audio somewhere. For instance, on the back of an analog mixing board, in addition to the main outputs, you may find outputs labeled Busses 1–8, and so on. You could run a cable going from these outputs to another device, such as an ADAT recorder or a hardware effects unit. In this way, anything sent to busses 1–8 would go to the external device, as well as your main outputs. That is only one example of how a bus could be used. The important concept is that a bus is a path used to send audio from one place to another.

There are a million ways you can use busses in your music. In our "Upbeat Rock" tune, we use busses to create and pan a slight echo on the bass part, which gives us a stereo image of a mono track. Busses can also be used to help conserve processing power.

Busses are a type of send, and each fader in the Mixing Board has a group of four sends. The horizontal bar displays the selected send, designating where the audio will be sent. To set a bus as a destination, drag down to "New Bundle," and select the desired destination, such as "bus 1."

Accompanying each send is a knob , which determines how much of the signal will be sent to the destination. This knob is currently set to –∞, which is located around 7 o'clock. At –∞, no signal will be sent to the send destination. A value of – 0 dB is located at 2 o'clock . With this setting, the entire original signal will be sent to the send destination. The original signal will not increase or decrease. At 5 o'clock is +6 dB . Use this setting with great caution. Remember, this will boost the signal 6 dB. If your original signal peaked at –2 dB, your boosted signal will go over 0 dB and distortion will result.

In summary, the send determines the destination of the signal, while the send knob determines what percentage of the original signal goes to that destination.

SHORTCUT Double-clicking or Ctrl-clicking on a send knob will set it to 0 dB.
Option-clicking on a send knob will set its stereo pair to the same setting.

In this example, the audio is being sent to bus 1 and bus 2. The send amount is relatively low. If you wish to quickly turn off a send, you can use the mute buttons in the middle.

FIGURE 11.11 Busses 1 and 2

USING BUSSES WITH EFFECTS

FIGURE 11.12 Bass Bus Settings for "Upbeat Rock"

In chapter 5, we discussed aux tracks primarily in the context of "virtual cables," allowing you to route audio from one place to another. Notably, while the audio signal is in route, you can apply effects. Aux tracks can access the same collection of audio plug-ins as audio tracks.

In figure 11.12, look at the track named "Bass Echo." It is an Aux track with a "bus 1" input and an "Analog 1–2" output. This will route any audio from bus 1 to Analog 1–2. In addition, the "Bass Echo" track also contains an "Echo" effect. The result: any audio located at bus 1 will be routed to Analog 1–2 along with an echo.

FIGURE 11.13 Echo Set to "Bass Echo" Track. This will create a 30 ms echo.

In figure 11.13 you can see the Echo contains one delay, at 30 ms. Since the mix is 100%, this plug-in will output only the processed signal: the echo effect. This echo goes on to the output of the aux track (Analog 1–2).

Now look at the Bass track in figure 11.12. Using its sends, it is routing its signal to bus 1. With this setup, the Bass track contains the original audio signal and sends it to Analog 1–2 via its output. Simultaneously, the signal is sent to bus 1 via its audio send, and thus to the aux track, Bass Echo. The aux track delays the signal 30 ms and then sends it on to Analog 1–2.

Conveniently, this places the original signal and the processed signal on independent faders that each have their own volume and panning settings. In this case, the Bass track is panned left while the Bass Echo track is panned right. The result is a fuller, stereo image of the original mono signal.

USING BUSSES TO REDUCE CPU LOAD

You can also use internal routing to organize your effects and save computer-processing power. It is very common to put reverb on multiple tracks, and the temptation is to insert a reverb on each individual track. This technique will work, but it may load down your system. However, consider the setup in figure 11.14.

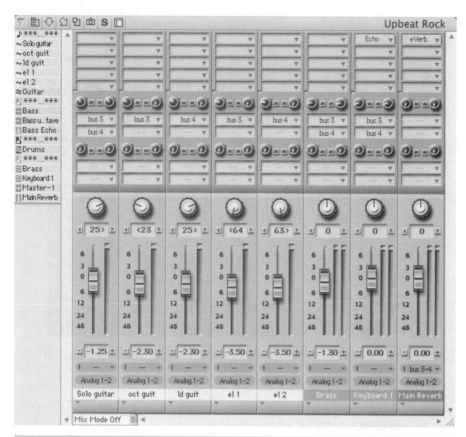

FIGURE 11.14 Bus Reducing CPU Load. All parts are sent to a single eVerb plug-in.

In figure 11.14, there is one aux track named "Main Reverb." It contains the eVerb plug-in, and its inputs are bus 3–4. This means anything sent to bus 3–4 will produce reverb. Next, the guitar, brass, and keyboard tracks are sent to bus 3–4, resulting in reverb. You can control the amount of reverb by the amount you initially send. For instance, more of the Solo Guitar track than the Keyboard 1 is sent to bus 3–4 , resulting in more reverb on the guitar.

Be aware that bus 3–4 is a stereo image. Accordingly, anything sent to bus 3 will be treated as a left signal and to bus 4 will be treated as a right signal. Now, consider the track named "El 1." This is a rhythm guitar track that is panned hard left. Since we would also want the reverb to be hard left, it is sent to only bus 3. Likewise, the "El 2" track, which is panned hard right, is sent only to bus 4.

Audio plug-ins are notorious for taking up processing power and slowing down computers. The setup above will result in a smoother running machine than individual eVerbs on every track, because your computer only needs to calculate reverb in one spot. If the eVerb plug-in was placed on every track, your computer would be calculating reverb seven times, unnecessarily taxing your processor.

11.7 Track Groups

After creating our bass echo effect, it would be desirable to group the bass tracks, allowing us to treat them as one element. For instance, we may decide to raise or lower the overall level of the bass. To do so, we would need to raise or lower *both* the "Bass" and "Bass Echo" tracks. If we group the tracks, both faders will move when one is moved.

In my mix of "Upbeat Rock," there are, in fact, three bass tracks. The first is the original bass, the second is the echoed bass, and the third is the original bass transposed up an octave. This higher bass will act as the bass element on smaller speaker systems that cannot produce lower pitches, such as typical computer or television speakers.

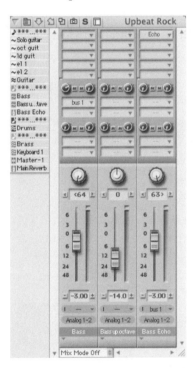

FIGURE 11.15 Submix of Three Basses

In figure 11.15, the levels are set so that the original signal and the echo are at the same volume, with the transposed signal at a lower level. This kind of grouping is called a "submix." A *submix* is an independent mix of several elements within your larger, final mix. When you have a submix you like, you can group these tracks so that if you move one fader they all move together, preserving their relative values.

To create a track group, highlight the desired tracks, and choose Project Menu–Modify Track Groups–New Track Group. Give it an appropriate name, and click OK.

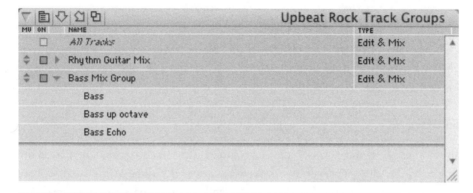

FIGURE 11.16 Bass Track Group

In figure 11.16, you can see there are two current track groups: one for the bass tracks and another for the rhythm guitar tracks. Also, notice that both group types are "Edit & Mix." This means that, just as the faders move together, when you cut or trim soundbites, they will move together.

Switching the "Type" to "Custom" allows you to group different attributes for the tracks.

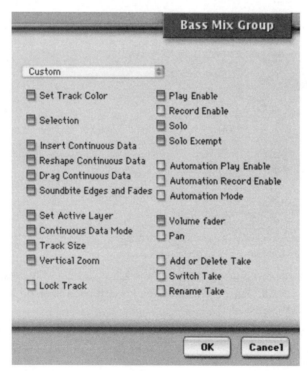

FIGURE 11.17 Custom Type Window

For example, in this Custom setting, the volume faders, play enables, and solos are grouped, while the automation features are not.

11.8 Automation Snapshot

An *automation snapshot* is a saved set of Mixing Board settings. You can use it to set your MIDI gear to the appropriate starting parameters (e.g., volume, panning).

When you are working with MIDI tracks, remember that the overall volume is ultimately determined by the volume setting on your sound module. On MIDI tracks, the Mixing Board's volume fader is merely a means to send volume settings to your sound modules. For instance, if you are using a track assigned to XV-3080/3, when you move the fader to 104, a MIDI message is sent from your computer to the MIDI interface and on to the XV-3080. This message will indicate your wish to change the volume setting of channel 3 to 104. *The location of the fader is irrelevant unless this information physically is sent to your sound modules.*

When you move a fader up or down, this information is sent to your sound modules. The act of *changing* a fader triggers the message, not the fader's starting position. However, by using automation snapshots, it is possible to print (save) this information on your actual MIDI tracks. Then, when the cursor passes this information during playback, it is sent on to your sound modules.

If you do not do one of these two things, you are not controlling volume settings on your sound module. For instance, let's say that on "Upbeat Rock," you set your volumes perfectly and save your file. Then, you open another project you are working on, called "Sentimental Ballad." At the end of "Sentimental Ballad," each MIDI track fades out, setting the volume parameters on your sound modules to zero.

Then, you return to "Upbeat Rock." You open the file and click play—but you do not hear any of your MIDI tracks. This is because the volume settings on your sound modules are still set to zero.

To retain your mix of "Upbeat Rock," you could then open the Mixing Board, moving each track up and down the same amount, which is tedious and a waste of time. Instead, you could make an Automation Snapshot, and print the settings of your Mixing Board to each track. Then, when you click Play, these settings will be sent to your sound modules. Obviously, using an Automation Snapshot is much quicker.

TAKING THE SNAPSHOT

To take an Automation Snapshot, move the cursor to where you want the data to be saved, and click the Snapshot icon in the Mixing Board.

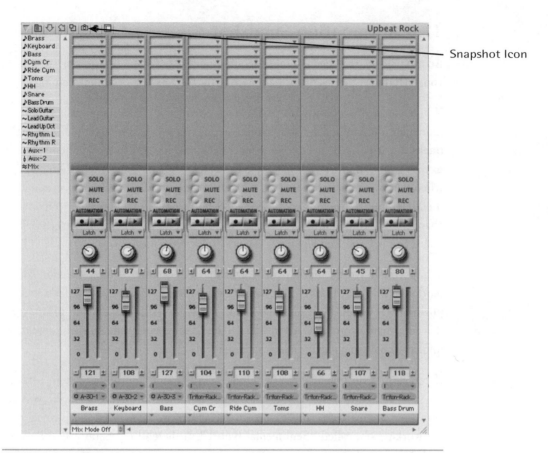

Snapshot Icon

FIGURE 11.18 Snapshot Icon

After doing so, you will get the Automation Snapshot Window.

Automation Snapshot

Time Range: All Time

Tracks: Tracks Shown in Mixing Board

Data Types: Data Types Visible in Mixing Board

Command key bypasses dialog   OK   Cancel

FIGURE 11.19 Automation Snapshot Window

Here you can designate the preferences of your snapshot. The first element is "Time Range." Remember that taking a snapshot prints information about volumes, and so on, onto your tracks. The Time Range designates where this information will be printed. "All Time" is selected here, meaning that the information will be printed over the entire sequence. In reality, this means the information will be placed at the very beginning and then never altered. But be careful, if you have already put volume changes in your sequence (such as crescendos). "All Time" will erase them. If you have already made volume changes throughout your sequence, choose a different time range. Since we have not done so yet, "All Time" is the preferred choice.

Next, you must choose which tracks are affected. "Tracks Shown in Mixing Board" is currently selected. This is why the automation was printed on only the tracks we were using, rather than every track.

Then, you must choose what information from your Mixing Board will be printed onto your tracks. "Data Types Visible in Mixing Board" is currently chosen. This means every element in the Mixing Board—volume, pan, record-enable, play/mute, solo, bussing, effects—will be printed onto each track, but other possible automation data will not be printed.

When your preferences are set, click OK. Now, the information will appear in your Sequence Editor.

In the following file, notice how the first measure is blank on all of the MIDI tracks.

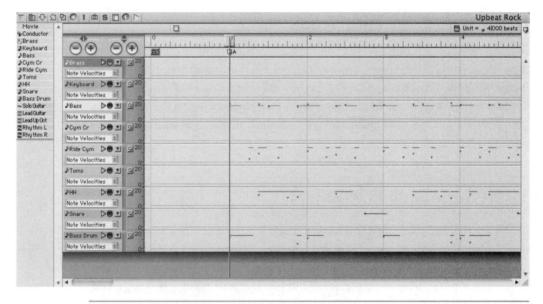

FIGURE 11.20 Tracks Before Snapshot

After taking the snapshot, measure 0 is filled with data.

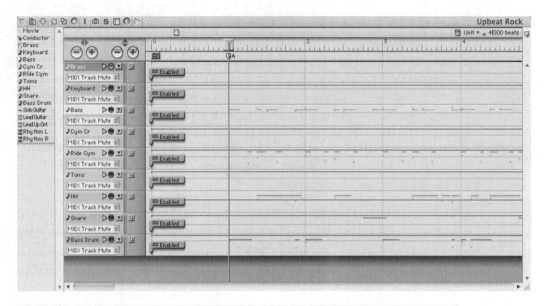

FIGURE 11.21 Tracks Including Snapshot

This snapshot contains all the information about how your Mixing Board is set up, including volumes, pannings, reverb plug-ins, track mutes, and so on.

PLAY-ENABLING THE AUTOMATION

Digital Performer will only use the volume and panning settings on your tracks if the automation is play-enabled. You can play-enable the automation in the Mixing Board by clicking the Automation Play button ▶ for each track. For audio tracks, this also can be done in the Track Information Panel by clicking on the "Auto" row Auto ⬍. When this button is green, all is right in the universe, and your automation settings will be in effect.

11.9 Continuous Controllers

Continuous controllers are MIDI messages designed to change data smoothly over time. Unlike a Note On message, where one message triggers an easily defined object (a note), in a continuous controller action, such as gradually increasing the volume or bending a pitch, many events (generally, in tiny increments) may be sent, giving the illusion of a gradual change.

If we look at the Event List for the Bass track, you can see there is new information at 0|1|000. The first event indicates that continuous controller #10 (pan) is set to 64. The second indicates that continuous controller #7 (volume) is set to 118. The third indicates that the track is play-enabled. This information was printed here by our snapshot.

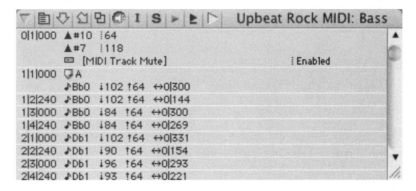

FIGURE 11.22 Event List Showing Continuous Controller Information

There are many continuous controllers. Some are standardized across different brands of MIDI products, and some are unassigned. The most commonly used include:

#1 Modulation—Typically adds a vibrato effect, but this can vary.

#5 Portamento Time—The speed at which a portamento slides between two pitches.

#7 Volume—The level of the sound.

#10 Pan—The left/right location of the sound.

#11 Expression—A subset of Volume.

#64 Sustain Pedal—Simulates the sustain pedal of a piano.

#66 Sostenuto Pedal—Simulates the sostenuto pedal of a grand piano.

#67 Soft Pedal—Simulates the soft pedal of a piano.

#68 Legato Pedal—Creates a legato effect, as if a wind player did not tongue an attack.

#72 Release Time—Determines the length of a sound's release.

#73 Attack Time—Determines the length of a sound's attack.

#74 Brightness—Affects the timbre of a sound, similar to a low pass EQ.

The effect of these messages will vary, depending on your setup. You are not guaranteed that any given controller will produce the expected effect. The message itself simply states a controller number and a value, such as #11 and 64. It is up to the receiving device, most likely your sound module, to determine what each controller number does to the sound. Many sound modules will simply ignore some of the less common controllers. Other effects will vary, depending upon the patch. For instance, modulation may introduce a vibrato on a flute patch, while introducing an arpeggio on a synth patch.

Continuous controllers and automation are two terms commonly mistaken for one another. Continuous controllers describes a particular type of MIDI Message, while automation describes the act of using continuous controllers and other MIDI Messages to record movements throughout your sequence.

11.10 Using Continuous Controllers

By now, you may have guessed you can use continuous controller #7 (volume) to create dynamics throughout your sequence. Let's return to the expanded version of the keyboard part of our "Upbeat Rock." In the "Pad" track, there is a crescendo starting at measure 9 and ending at measure 13.

The most intuitive way to create this effect is in the Mixing Board. Next to the Automation Play-Enable button is a Record button.

FIGURE 11.23 Automation Record and Play

Let's create the volume information for a track by using the automation features in the Mixing Board. First, click the Record Automation button, so that it turns red. Second, rewind to the beginning of your sequence, and click Play. Then third, during playback, move the volume fader.

When you are done recording, press Stop and disarm the Record button. By doing this, you have recorded the fader movements.

Using this method, I have created a crescendo in the pad part. We can view this crescendo in the Sequence Editor. On the Pad track, a new edit layer for volume is created. Here, we can see the crescendo. Volume starts at 0 at measure 9 and ends at 86 in measure 13.

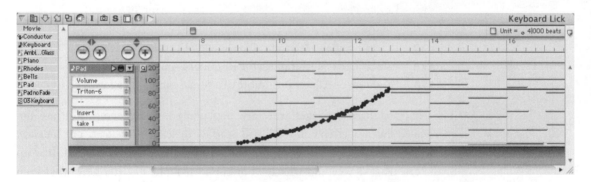

FIGURE 11.24 Volume Crescendo Curve. Line Mode.

In figure 11.24, the volume curve is shown as a line with a series of data points. You can view continuous controller data in the Sequence Editor in several ways. These options do not effect how the controller data acts in any way. They are merely for your visual preference.

To set your preference, click on the Track Information Menu. Figure 11.25 shows how to view the volume data as "points."

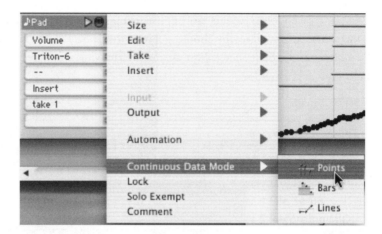

FIGURE 11.25 Displaying Automation Data

In "Point" mode, our Pad volume graph appears as shown in figure 11.26.

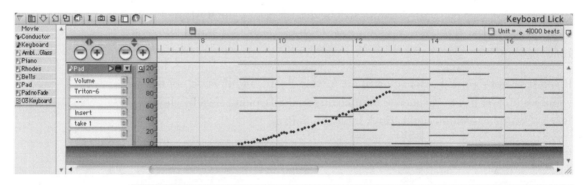

FIGURE 11.26 Point Mode

In "Bars" mode, our Pad volume graph appears as shown in figure 11.27.

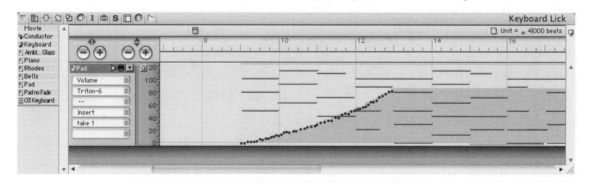

FIGURE 11.27 Bar Mode

Although recording volume automation in the Mixing Board is often effective, you may sometimes want to input/edit the data in greater detail. Once a volume edit layer is created, you can make precise changes in the Sequence Editor.

Let's even out our crescendo so that it is more consistent. First, switch the cursor to the Pencil tool (shortcut: Double-p), by choosing it from the Tools Palette (shortcut: Shift-o). Then, drag in the Sequence Editor so you are drawing a new crescendo. The result is a smooth crescendo.

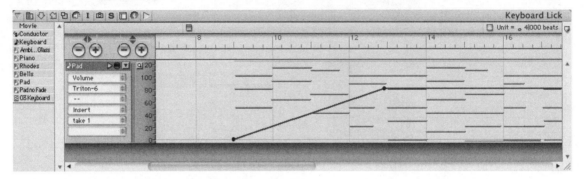

FIGURE 11.28 Editing Volume in the Sequence Editor

Remember, the shape of what you draw will be determined by the Reshape Flavor in the Tools Palette. The crescendo in figure 11.28 was achieved with a "Straight Line" reshape.

If you have not recorded automation in the Mixing Board, and thus do not have a volume edit layer in your Sequence Editor, you can draw volume data by choosing Insert–Controller–Volume in the Track Information Panel.

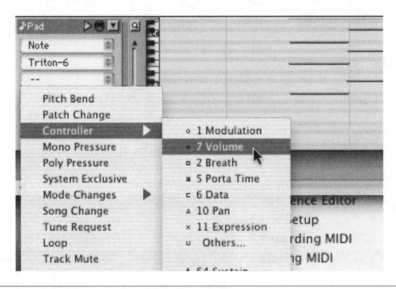

FIGURE 11.29 Adding a Volume Layer

In addition to recording fader movements in the Mixing Board or drawing volume changes in the Sequence Editor, we could also create this crescendo from the Region menu. Begin by selecting the measures and tracks you want affected, in this case measures 9–13 of the "Pad" track. Next, choose Region–Create Continuous Data.

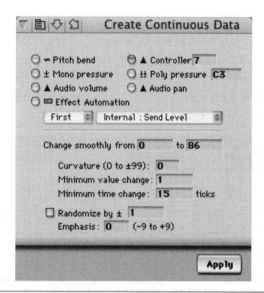

FIGURE 11.30 Create Continuous Data Window

In figure 11.30, we are telling Digital Performer to create Controller #7 (volume) and "change smoothly from 0 to 86." This will create a volume curve that changes from zero (at the beginning of our selection) to 86 (at the end of our selection).

EXPRESSION VERSUS VOLUME

Expression (#11) is a continuous controller setting that works in conjunction with volume to create phrasing and other subtler volume variations within a volume region. Think of expression as a percentage of volume, on a scale of 0 to 127, where 0 is 0% of the volume setting and 127 as 100% of the volume setting.

Volume	Expression	Combined Effect
127	127 (100%)	127
127	64 (50%)	64
86	64 (50%)	43
86	0 (0%)	0

This gives you two controllers to affect overall volume and makes certain tasks much easier. Before the Expression controller, we had to use volume to control two separate things: the mixing levels and the internal dynamics used to shape phrases. This can cause inconveniences.

For instance, let's say you are writing a four-minute cue for a film score. It is a heart-wrenching moment, with lots of strings fading in and out. You've used volume to make all of your swells. When you play it for the director, he says, "I love everything, but could we make the cellos a little bit louder?" You say, "Sure," and then have to deal with four minutes worth of detailed volume curves.

Now, let's rewind and assume you used Expression to create all those heart-wrenching swells. Then, you place one volume controller at the beginning to reflect the mix, perhaps with a snapshot. When the director asks you to raise the overall level of the cellos, you can do so by simply raising one volume controller at the beginning. When this controller is raised, the Expression fades in the rest of the track remain intact.

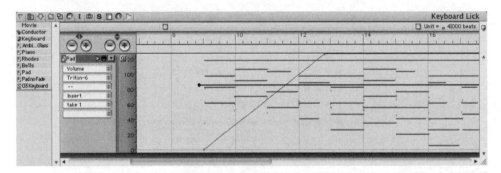

TRACK 9

FIGURE 11.31 Volume and Expression Controllers

In figure 11.31, Expression and Volume are used in conjunction to create the crescendo in the Pad track. Here, an overall volume is set at 86. Then an Expression curve goes from 0 to 127 (0% to 100%). This creates the same result as a volume curve from 0 to 86, but separates the functions of mixing and phrasing.

11.11 Creating Dynamics on Audio Tracks

Volume data on audio tracks is classified as "Audio Volume." While this is not continuous controller data, you can create Audio Volume data the same way you did on MIDI tracks: by recording fader movements in the Mixing Board or drawing curves in the Sequence Editor. Expression does not exist for audio tracks.

As with MIDI tracks, the automation must be play-enabled. If it is not play-enabled on audio tracks, the volume graph will appear as a dotted line, and it will not have any playback effect.

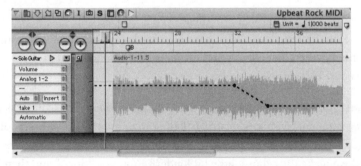

FIGURE 11.32 A Dotted Line Reveals Disabled Automation Playback

11.12 Master Fader

If you are using a large number of audio tracks, you may find a Master Fader track useful. Like other tracks, master fader tracks are created from Digital Performer's Project menu. Once created, you can place volume changes on a master fader track just as you would an audio track—either in the Mixing Board or the Sequence Editor. These volume changes will be applied to every audio track that has the same output as the master fader track.

P08
MASTER
FADER

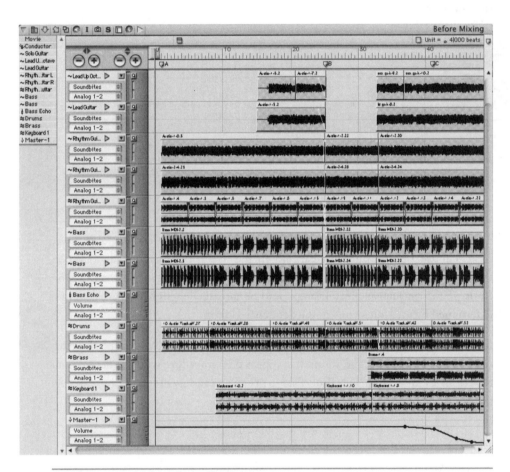

FIGURE 11.33 Master Fader Track

Figure 11.33 shows "Upbeat Rock" with only audio. The Master-1 track is a master fader track that is used to control Analog 1–2, which happens to include all of our tracks. A fade is defined on the Master Fader starting at measure 39. The result? All tracks will fade together, creating the "Repeat and Fade" effect.

11.13 Additional Automation

MIDI

In addition to volume, you can automate nearly any kind of MIDI or audio message. Let's return to the expanded keyboard part. Here, the Sequence Editor is open for the keyboard part, and a lot of pan data has been added. This particular effect will cause the track to pan from left to right, arriving at each extreme on the downbeat of each measure.

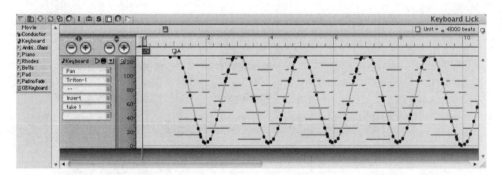

FIGURE 11.34 Automating Panning on a MIDI Track

To accomplish this, switch the Reshape Flavor in the Tools Palette to a sine wave. Next, choose Insert–Controller–Pan On in the Track Information Panel. When the Pencil appears, draw to your heart's delight. If you use a cyclical shape in the Reshape Flavor, such as Sine, Triangle, and Square, the length of one cycle will be determined by the Unit setting in the Sequence Editor.

In this manner, you can create any kind of continuous controller data: pitch bend, modulation, brightness, and so on. Just repeat this procedure with a different data type from the Insert row. The Tools Palette provides a variety of Insert Curve shapes for you to choose from.

AUDIO

As with MIDI, you can also automate panning on audio tracks. The process is the same as audio volume, except you select Pan `Pan` instead of Volume `Volume`. In figure 11.35, a similar panning effect is applied to the rhythm guitars in "Upbeat Rock." Remember, the automation must be play-enabled.

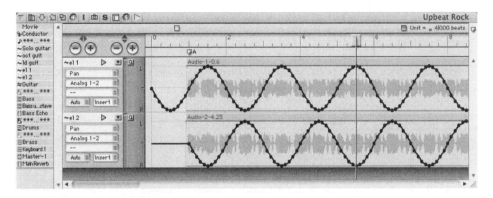

FIGURE 11.35 Automating Panning on an Audio Track

In addition, you can automate any settings of audio plug-ins. In the following example, a Low-Pass EQ has been placed on the rhythm guitar tracks. The frequency cutoff has been automated to create a sweep affect.

To do this, first open the plug-in you wish to automate. In this case, it is the 4-band EQ.

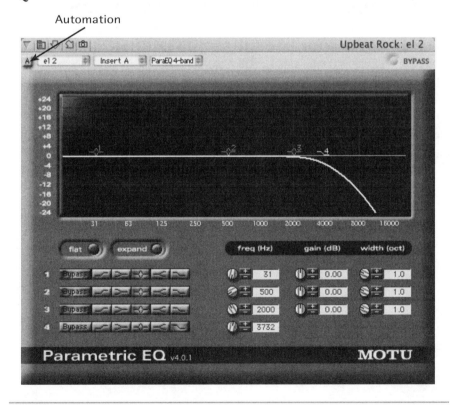

FIGURE 11.36 EQ, Automation Play-enabled

Begin by record-enabling the automation. You can do this in the Mixing Board, as we did with MIDI tracks. Also, you can do this in each plug-in by clicking on the "A" in the upper-left-hand corner and choosing Record. When ready to record, the "A" will display red.

Rewind, and click Play in your sequencer. During playback, move the EQ settings you wish to automate.

These EQ changes will show up in the Sequence Editor on the appropriate audio track. As with all other automation, you can edit or write this data with the Pencil tool.

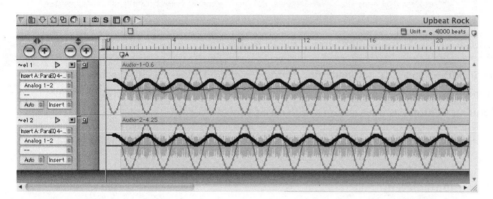

FIGURE 11.37 Automated EQ Curves

Mixing from within Digital Performer provides a range of advantages. You can complete all of the basic mixing functions, such as setting levels and panning. You can utilize multiple software effects, which would require many expensive hardware devices. You can graphically see and edit your automation. To top it off, all of these settings are automatically saved with your file and recalled instantly.

MUSICAL CONSIDERATIONS

12.1 MIDIstration

We have all heard complaints about MIDI music. I remember a client saying, "You're not going to use one of those twinky synthesizers are you?" When I sent him the music, he loved it and thought that it was a live rock band. This illustrates both the power of contemporary sequencing technology and the mindset of some potential clients.

These days, getting realistic sounding performances from a MIDI setup like Digital Performer is achieved much more easily than it had been in the past. But there are some important techniques that you must use, if you wish to create convincing performances.

One technique is what I like to call *MIDIstration*—the act of orchestrating for your MIDI equipment. This includes the act of selecting patches, combining sounds, and more.

SIMULATING A LIVE PERFORMANCE

There are essentially two kinds of MIDI projects. The first is when the MIDI acts as a substitute for an acoustic performance. For instance, you may decide not to hire an entire orchestra, choosing instead to replicate the orchestra as best you can. Similarly, the MIDI performance can act as a sketch or demo for elements that ultimately will be recorded by a live ensemble. For instance, you may sequence a saxophone solo, knowing all along you will eventually replace it with a live performance. The second kind of MIDI project involves the MIDI as its own legitimate genre. Many genres are produced entirely with MIDI, with no intention of imitating or utilizing a live performance.

When simulating a live performance, the first step is to invest in the best sound sources you can afford. Sampling libraries are expensive, but the composer who gets hired is often the composer with the best samples rather than the composer with the best writing skills. Of course, expensive sound sources do not guarantee a great sequence either. So, after you get the best sounds you can reasonably afford, what next?

The short answer is to analyze the original sounds of the instruments you are imitating, in a very detailed manner, and then imitate it. First, consider the range of the acoustic instrument you are recreating. For instance, most flutes cannot play below middle C. If you venture below this C when sequencing a flute part, your sequence will no longer sound like a flute. While the result may be interesting, it will not be an accurate reflection of a flute. Also, examine how the range affects dynamics and tone color. In the case of a flute, it is extremely difficult to play quietly in the high register. Therefore, your flute track should increase in volume when it goes to the flute's high register.

Also, consider a trumpet part. Like flutists, trumpet players use extra airspeed to create higher pitches, simultaneously raising the overall volume. In addition, a loud trumpet part has a much brighter sound than a soft trumpet part. In addition to the range and dynamics, this tone color must be replicated. You may simulate this brightness by increasing velocities or selecting a bright trumpet patch.

In addition to range and tone color, listen to the original sound in terms of attack and decay. The *attack* is the beginning of a pitch. The *decay* is its duration. Some instruments will be relatively simple to analyze and imitate. For instance, if you play a note on the piano, it will decay at a predictable rate. Of course, the attack will vary greatly depending on how hard the key was struck. In MIDI, the attacks can be simulated with varying velocities and the decay will be programmed into the patch. Other instruments will be much more complex. Consider a clarinet. When a clarinetist plays a note, he can use a loud or soft attack. While sustaining, he can crescendo, decrescendo, add vibrato, play straight tone, bend the pitch, and so on. These possibilities must be programmed into your sequence, with velocity, volume, expression, modulation, pitch bend, and so on.

Most commonly, your MIDI performance will be played on a keyboard. One common mistake is to perform in a manner that is possible on your keyboard, but not on the acoustic instrument you are imitating. For instance, a trumpet cannot sound more than one note at a time, while your MIDI keyboard can. Likewise, a drummer has only two hands. While this is usually enough for most practical purposes, it does not enable the drummer to hit the crash cymbal, hi-hats, toms, and snare drum simultaneously. Be sure that your MIDI performance is true to the capabilities of the acoustic instruments and performers, if you are trying to replicate an acoustic sound.

Does the acoustic performance consist of a soloist or a section? In an orchestra, there is usually one English horn player per part, while there may be fifteen violinists per part. This fact should be replicated in your sequence. When selecting patches, choose appropriate ones. If you are creating a string section, choose "Full Strings" in favor of "Solo Violin." In addition, do not limit yourself to one MIDI track per part. Layering "Full Strings," "Bright Strings" and "Arco Violins" with slightly different performances on each track will produce a better section sound than any one track alone.

Last, go to a concert. We have a tendency to sit behind our rigs so much that the sound modules become the "real thing." They are not. From time to time, use the Shutdown feature on your computer, and go hear your local orchestra or rock band. Let it inspire you.

12.2 Layering

Not all sequencing imitates acoustic performances. In this case, what considerations can you make, while sequencing, to improve your music?

First, do not limit yourself to one track per part. Layering complimentary sounds will give your sequences a full, multidimensional sound. In addition, by combining patches, you are quite likely to come up with a unique sound—one that does not readily exist on your sound module.

If we look at the keyboard part in "Upbeat Rock," it is nothing more than a TB-303 sound playing arpeggios on the chord progression: B♭ | D♭ | A♭ | E♭. This is fine, but layering some additional sounds can give this idea a bit more life.

TRACK 12

P09
EMBELLISHMENT

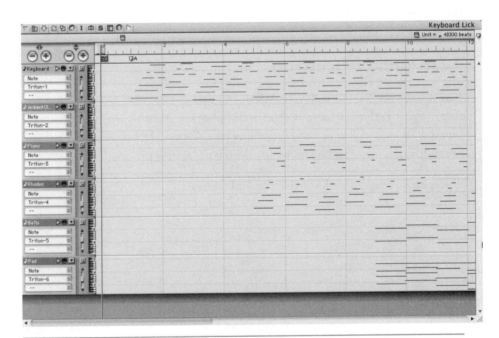

FIGURE 12.1 Layering of Keyboard Sounds

In this example, we have the keyboard passage alone for four measures. At measure 5, a piano and a Rhodes join in. They are essentially doubling the part, but rather than playing the entire lick, the Rhodes plays the first two beats of each measure and the piano plays the second two in tag-team fashion. This is a common effect. Rather than playing a part of steady eighth notes in one track, pass the idea around from one patch to another. The change of color is interesting to the ear. With this effect layered on top of the original part, the piano and Rhodes act essentially as "ear candy," sweetening the original part.

At measure 9, notice the bells come in. Again, they are essentially doubling the original keyboard part. However, rather than playing every note, they are only playing on the downbeats. This is another effective technique. Pick the notes in the part you wish to highlight, and double them with an additional color.

Also at measure 9, a sustained pad begins to play quietly in the background. Again, the pitches are the same as the original keyboard part, but rather than taking the form of a rhythmic arpeggio, they are sustained chords. This adds a great deal of depth to the track.

These concepts are by no means new. Just as a classical composer will pass a motive around an orchestra, we can pass a melody from sound module to sound module. Just as a jazz band will add brass stabs to highlight certain points in a melody, we can highlight certain points with additional patches. The end result will be lively and interesting sequences.

12.3 Audio Processing

Just as there are ways to craft your MIDI, you can also be creative with your audio data. Digital Performer has a host of audio plug-ins. Most of Digital Performer's plug-ins are intended to be used for mixing (see chapter 11), but some can be used to create variations of audio files for use during the writing process.

These audio plug-ins are located in the Audio menu.

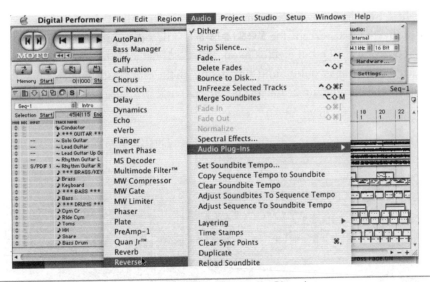

FIGURE 12.2 Accessing Digital Performer's Audio Plug-Ins

To process an audio file with a plug-in, highlight the soundbite in the Sequence Editor. Then choose the desired plug-in from the audio menu. Using plug-ins in this manner is "constructive" editing. *Constructive editing* results in the creation of a new file. This new file is placed in your audio files folder and replaces the previous soundbite in your Digital Performer project, but the previous audio file is preserved on your hard drive.

Using these tools, you can create effects that would otherwise be musically impossible. In the following file, various audio elements have been processed to create a variation of "Upbeat Rock." The drums have been converted to audio and placed on three stereo tracks. The guitar lick has been spliced and placed in every other measure.

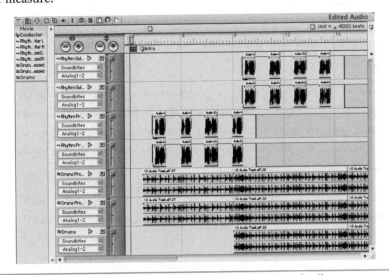

FIGURE 12.3 "Upbeat Rock" with MIDI Tracks Recorded to Audio

The first two drum tracks contain very drastic EQs. All of the frequencies are drastically reduced, except for 1865, a B-flat. The other processed drum track contains a similar EQ, but it zeros in on 932, the B-flat an octave lower. B-flat was chosen so the drums would sound "in pitch" with the other instruments. This effect is used in the introduction, while the full drums come in at measure 9.

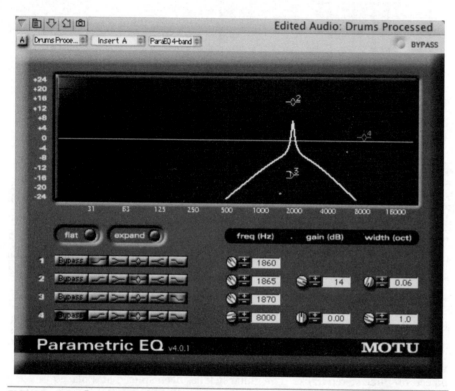

FIGURE 12.4 Parametric EQ

In the guitar, each measure has been processed using the Multimode Filter and an EQ. The processed files are placed every other measure so that they alternate with the original signal.

In addition to the audio plug-ins, you can also transpose audio (Region Menu) and apply *spectral effects* (Audio Menu). With these tools, you can take one audio file and create countless variations. These variations can then be layered and alternated, fading in and out. Yes, this is a different creative process than writing a pop song or a fugue, but a valid one in its own right.

I would encourage you simply to experiment and be creative. Just as MIDIstration will liven up your sequences, audio processing will give your tracks a fresh and unique sound.

PRINTING YOUR FINAL MIX

13.1 Recording Your Mix

Exactly how you route the audio to record your final mix will depend greatly on how your studio is set up. At what point should your tracks combine to become one stereo signal? If you are using a mid-range setup, this will occur at your external mixing board. Run appropriate audio cables from your mixing board to your audio interface. For instance, you may have a digital mixing board and can run an S/PDIF cable from your board to your interface. Then, create a stereo audio track, set its input to S/PDIF 1–2, and record.

If your setup is without an external mixer, all of your audio is already located at your audio interface. In figure 13.1, all of the audio outputs are set to Analog 1–2. This includes all Aux tracks, audio tracks, and instrument tracks. Likewise, this is all of the audio produced in our piece, meaning our final mix is currently being sent to output Analog 1–2.

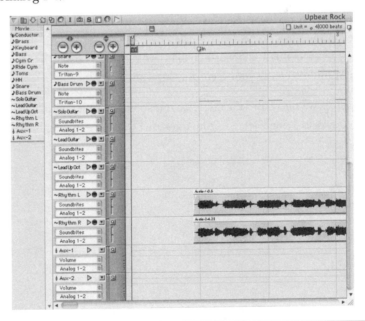

FIGURE 13.1 "Upbeat Rock." All audio routed to Analog 1–2.

In figure 13.2, all of these outputs have been switched to Bus 1–2. Now, our final mix is being routed to Bus 1–2. In this case, you can think of Bus 1–2 as an internal storage place, to which you can send and retrieve audio.

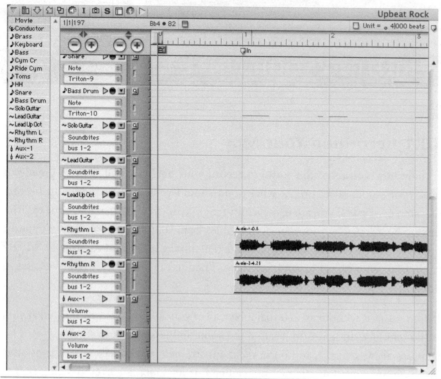

FIGURE 13.2 Routing to Bus 1–2

Because our final mix is located at Bus 1–2, we can record our mix on a single stereo track by recording Bus 1–2. To do so, create a new stereo track, give it an appropriate name, set its input to Bus 1–2, record-enable, and record. As usual, be sure to check the Audio Monitor to verify your recording level and drive location.

With this setup, we can record the mix from our sound modules, virtual instruments, and audio tracks to a single stereo audio track—all without a mixing board.

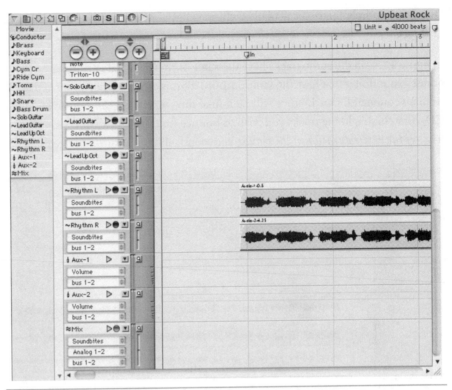

FIGURE 13.3 Recording to a Stereo Track

13.2 Bouncing to Disk

Bouncing is another way to combine several audio tracks into one audio file. Using the "Bounce to Disk" command, you can create useful submixes and even your final mix.

When creating a mix, bouncing is beneficial for two reasons. First, it occurs entirely in the digital realm; the new file is created entirely by internal calculations in the computer. This means there is no degradation of the audio quality. You can bounce 5,000 times, and the end result will still be as high quality as the original tracks. If you transfer from cassette to cassette 5,000 times, the end result will be distorted, with artifacts from the tape, and a loss of signal and fidelity.

Second, your computer can make these calculations faster than real-time recording. This speed will vary depending upon your computer, but on my system, I just bounced 1:05 of music in 12 seconds. This just saved 53 seconds—almost enough time to toast a bagel!

However, you cannot use Bounce to Disk in every situation. Most notably, Bounce to Disk will not record any MIDI elements. Remember, MIDI tracks send messages to external devices that, in turn, create the corresponding audio. Since Bounce to

Disk is an entirely internal calculation, these external MIDI devices are left out of the loop.

In figure 13.4, all the audio tracks have the same output. (Digital Performer can only bounce soundbites that have the same output.) This is a great opportunity to use the Bounce command. Our bounce will be a final mix, which we can put on an audio CD. First, highlight the tracks you wish to bounce (in this case, all of them). *Be sure to select the entire duration of the sequence.* Second, choose Audio–Bounce to Disk.

FIGURE 13.4 Soundbites to be Bounced

The Bounce to Disk window appears, where you need to provide some information. You are about to create a new audio file, so Digital Performer needs to know what the properties of that file will be.

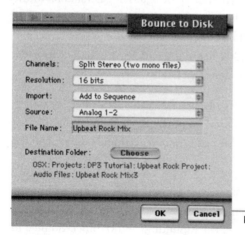

FIGURE 13.5 Bounce to Disk Window

1. Designate what format the audio file will be, in the "Channels" popup. In figure 13.5, "Split Stereo" has been selected, so a split-stereo audio file will be created. (If you are using the MOTU Audio System, you cannot create interleaved stereo audio files here.)

2. Choose the bit rate; 16-bit is chosen here.

3. Determine what Digital Performer should do with the new file(s) it is creating, by setting the "Import" popup.

   - With "Do Not Import," the file will be created and saved on your hard drive but not imported into your sequence.

   - With "Add to Soundbites Window," the file will be created on your hard drive and added to the Soundbites Window.

   - With "Add to Sequence," as selected here, the file will be created, added to the Soundbites Window, and placed on a new track in your sequence.

4. Designate which output to bounce. *Digital Performer can bounce only one output at a time.* In this example, every selected soundbite whose output is "Analog 1–2" will be included in the new file. If, for instance, the bass part was set to "Analog 3–4," it would not be included in the new file.

5. Choose a file name. To change the file name, click in the "File Name" field.

6. Designate the location of the audio file you are about to create. Digital Performer will give its best guess in the "Destination Folder" section. If you wish to change this, click "Choose," and locate your desired folder.

After clicking "OK," the file looks like figure 13.6. Notice that there is an entirely new track, "Mix." This track contains an audio file that is a composite of the other tracks. Any Mixing Board settings on these other tracks (such as reverbs, panning, delays, etc.) will be included in this new file/soundbite.

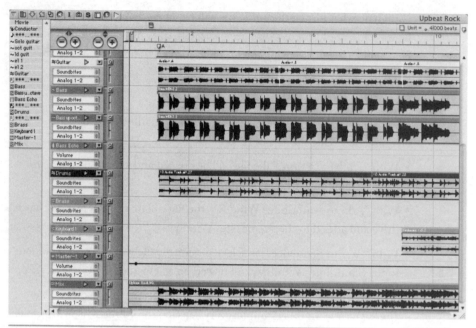

FIGURE 13.6 After Bounce Command. Notice the new track, Mix.

The new file is also listed in the Soundbites window. In figure 13.7, notice how the "Source" parameter of the audio file, "Upbeat Rock Mix," is listed as "Bounce To Disk." Also notice that there are other bounced tracks listed here, besides the final mix.

MUE	NAME	DURATION	SAMP RATE	FORMAT	SOURCE	FILE	DISK
∿	Audio-2-4.44	0:04.11	44100	16 Bit	Editing	Audio-2-4	OSX
∿	Bass MIDI-2.20	0:23.83	44100	16 Bit	Editing	Bass MIDI-2	OSX
∿	Bass MIDI-2.22	0:23.83	44100	16 Bit	Editing	Bass MIDI-2.P12	OSX
∿	Bass MIDI-2.23	0:11.63	44100	16 Bit	Editing	Bass MIDI-2	OSX
∿	Bass MIDI-2.24	0:11.63	44100	16 Bit	Editing	Bass MIDI-2.P12	OSX
∿	Bass MIDI-2.26	0:00.99	44100	16 Bit	Editing	Bass MIDI-2	OSX
∿	Bass MIDI-2.28	0:01.00	44100	16 Bit	Editing	Bass MIDI-2.P12	OSX
∿	Bass MIDI-2.3	0:35.67	44100	16 Bit	Editing	Bass MIDI-2	OSX
∿	Bass MIDI-2.5	0:35.67	44100	16 Bit	Editing	Bass MIDI-2.P12	OSX
≋	Brass-1.4	0:26.99	44100	16 Bit	Editing	Brass-1.L/R	OSX
≋	Keyboard 1-0.2	0:24.02	44100	16 Bit	Editing	Keyboard 1-0.L/R	OSX
≋	Keyboard 1-1.10	0:10.50	44100	16 Bit	Editing	Keyboard 1-1.L/R	OSX
≋	Keyboard 1-1.11	0:01.50	44100	16 Bit	Editing	Keyboard 1-1.L/R	OSX
≋	Keyboard 1-1.12	0:02.39	44100	16 Bit	Editing	Keyboard 1-1.L/R	OSX
≋	Keyboard 1-1.8	0:24.00	44100	16 Bit	Editing	Keyboard 1-1.L/R	OSX
∿	ld guit-8.2	0:25.23	44100	16 Bit	Editing	ld guit-8	OSX
∿	oct guit-10.2	0:19.85	44100	16 Bit	Editing	oct guit-10	OSX
∿	oct guit-9.2	0:06.37	44100	16 Bit	Editing	oct guit-9	OSX
∿	Rhythm Guitar L	1:15.12	44100	16 Bit	Bounce To Disk	Rhythm Guitar L	OSX
∿	Rhythm Guitar R	1:15.12	44100	16 Bit	Bounce To Disk	Rhythm Guitar R	OSX
≋	Upbeat Rock Mix	1:27.00	44100	16 Bit	Bounce To Disk	Upbeat Rock Mix2.L/R	OSX

FIGURE 13.7 Bounced Files in Soundbites Window

13.3 Mastering

Mastering is a process that occurs after you have created your final mixes. Mastering accomplishes several tasks. First, you can put finishing touches on the overall mix—such as EQ and compression—rather than on individual tracks. Typically, a mastering engineer will use compression and other dynamics to raise the overall level of the signal. This will allow it to sound at the same level as other commercial CDs. Second, a mastering engineer will also adjust the levels of each track in relation to each other throughout a CD. For instance, you may want the ballad to be quieter than the upbeat, opening track. The pauses between tracks can also be adjusted.

You can put finishing touches on the overall EQ and compression in Digital Performer's Soundbites window. So far, we have been using the Soundbites window in List mode [List]. The Soundbites Window also has an Info mode [Info], which shows more detailed information about the soundbite. Edit mode [Edit] allows you to edit the audio files. Unlike editing in the Sequence Editor, changes made in Edit mode are *destructive edits*. They alter the actual audio file on your hard drive.

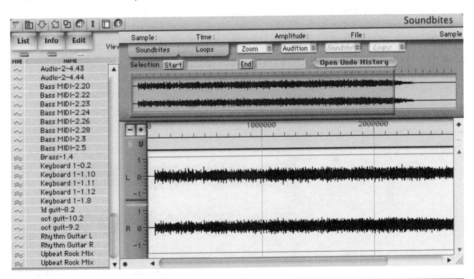

FIGURE 13.8 The Soundbite Window's Edit Mode

Figure 13.8 shows the "Upbeat Rock Mix" soundbite in Edit mode. A common desire is to *normalize* your mix. This function finds the loudest point in the audio file and increases the level at this point to 0 dB, also increasing everything else the same amount. For practical purposes, normalize increases an audio file to its loudest possible level, without creating distortion.

To do this in Digital Performer, you must be in Edit mode in the Soundbites window. Select your audio region by dragging the I-Beam cursor over it. Then choose Audio–Normalize. Figure 13.9 shows the waveform after its level has been raised.

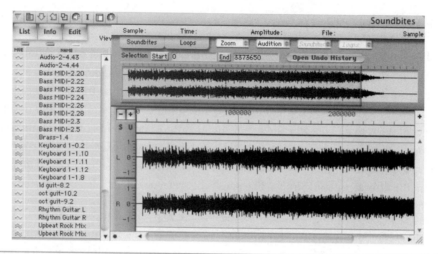

FIGURE 13.9 Normalized Waveform

In the Edit window, you can also use the "Fade-in" and "Fade-out" functions, as well as any of the plug-ins. Figure 13.10 shows a file that has been compressed with MW Compressor and a fade-in.

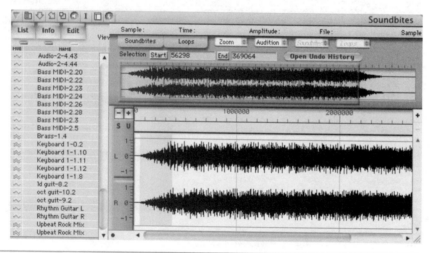

FIGURE 13.10 Compressed, and with a Fade-in

13.4 Exporting to AIFF

For stereo files, Digital Performer uses split-stereo Sound Designer II format. For each stereo file used in your sequence, there are actually two files on your hard drive. Both are mono; one is for the left speaker, while one is for the right. In figure 13.11, you can see that there are actually two files for "Upbeat Rock Mix." There is "Upbeat Rock Mix.L" and "Upbeat Rock Mix.R." Mono files, such as "oct guit-9," only occur once.

FIGURE 13.11 Stereo Files: R and L

This is fine while you are working in Digital Performer, but a single, composite, *interleaved-stereo* file is necessary when you want to put your final mix onto a CD. If split-stereo files are placed on a CD, the left channel becomes track 1 and the right channel becomes track 2—and both are mono. Obviously, this is not what we want. To have the complete stereo image, your audio files must be converted to an interleaved stereo format, such as AIFF.

You can convert your mix to AIFF in the Soundbites window. First, highlight the soundbite you wish to convert by clicking on the soundbite name. Second, choose "Export Selected Bites" from the mini-menu.

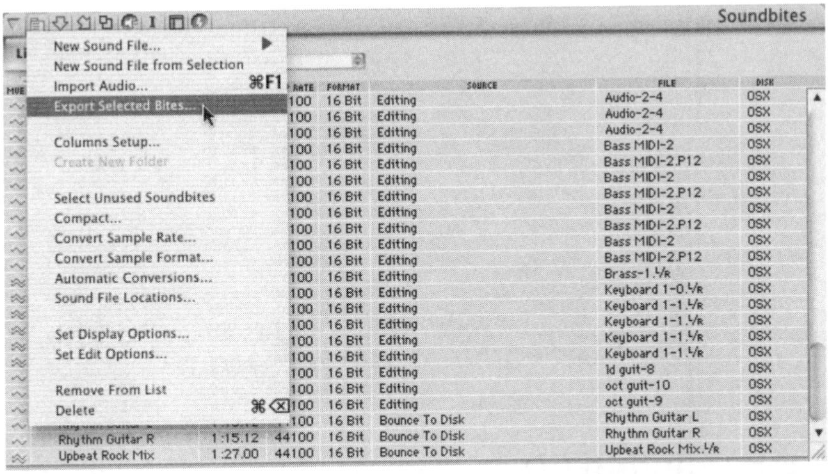

FIGURE 13.12 Exporting a Soundbite. This allows you to convert soundbites into interleaved stereo files, such as AIFF, which are suitable for audio CDs.

This creates a brand-new file, and prompts you to provide an appropriate name, drive location, and format. In figure 13.13, you can see that the new file will be located in the Audio Files folder for the "Upbeat Rock" project, called "Upbeat Rock Mix For CD," and formatted as an AIFF.

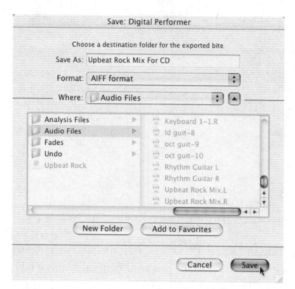

FIGURE 13.13 Saving as an AIFF

This exported AIFF file will show up as a single audio file. Notice in figure 13.14 that there is only one "Upbeat Rock Mix For CD" file. This is the stereo file that you would place on the CD.

FIGURE 13.14 Interleaved-Stereo File, Ready for Transfer to CD

13.5 Burning to CD

There are essentially two kinds of CD formats: audio and data. Audio CDs are the kind you use in your CD player to listen to music. Data CDs are the kind you use in your computer to store and load files. In this case, we are going to make an audio CD so that we can listen to this music with our CD player.

BURNING AN AUDIO CD

To burn your mix onto a CD, you will need a separate CD burning program. One of the most common in OSX is iTunes, which is free and part of the system software. When you insert a blank CDR into your writable CD drive, OSX will recognize that it is blank and ask you what you would like to do with it.

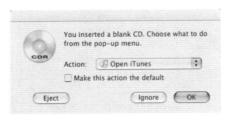

FIGURE 13.15 System Prompt for a Blank CD

In figure 13.15, we are opting to open iTunes, which is used to create audio CDs. Once in iTunes, you must create a new *playlist* (list of files to go onto your CD) in the file menu and give it an appropriate name. Then select the playlist and drag your AIFF files into the "Song Name" column.

Figure 13.16 shows that a new playlist titled "Upbeat Rock" has been created. The playlists are shown in the "Source" column. Next, two AIFF files have been added to the playlist: "Upbeat Rock" and "Keyboard Variation." This will produce an audio CD with two tracks on it. To create the CD, click on the "Burn Disc" icon in the upper right-hand corner of iTunes.

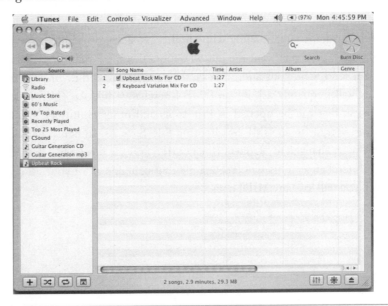

FIGURE 13.16 iTunes Window. The playlist "Upbeat Rock" is selected (Source), and there are two files ready to be burned onto the CD: the primary "Upbeat Rock" mix and a variation of this mix.

BURNING A DATA CD

If you wish to burn your Digital Performer sequence session to a data CD, you again begin by inserting a blank CDR. This time, choose "Open Finder."

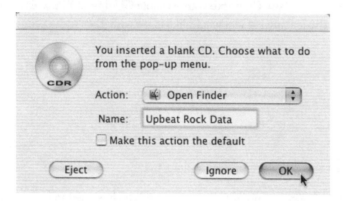

FIGURE 13.17 Burning a Data CD

When you click OK, the CD will show up on your desktop. Drag the files you wish to burn (such as your highest level "Upbeat Rock" folder) onto the CD. Last, drag the CD icon to the Trash, which will now display as a Burn Disc icon. This burns a data CD containing all of your files, which you could send to a peer or client.

13.6 Other Delivery Formats

CDs are the most common form of delivering music, but they are by no means the only kind. If you are collaborating with another musician, or sending your files to a mix engineer, they may want the files in a more flexible format than just a stereo mix. If you send them your audio tracks, they can mix it as they please. In such a case, they will frequently ask for an OMF Interchange file. An *OMF* is a generic audio format that can be opened in Pro Tools and other multitrack editors. You can convert you file to an OMF by choosing File–Save As. In figure 13.18, the file name has been changed to "Upbeat Rock OMF," and the format has been changed to OMF Interchange. This will create a file that contains all of your audio tracks. However, you will lose any MIDI data.

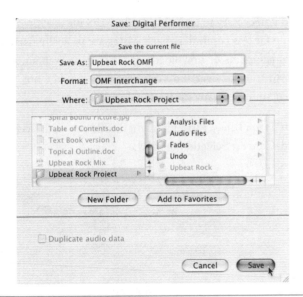

FIGURE 13.18 Converting to an OMF

There is also a file format called "SMF" (Standard MIDI File). This is a generic MIDI file, which can be opened in any MIDI program, such as Finale, Reason, or Logic. Again, begin by selecting File–Save As. In figure 13.19, the name has been changed to "Upbeat Rock MID," and the format has been changed to Standard MIDI File. This creates a file of your MIDI tracks, but not your audio data.

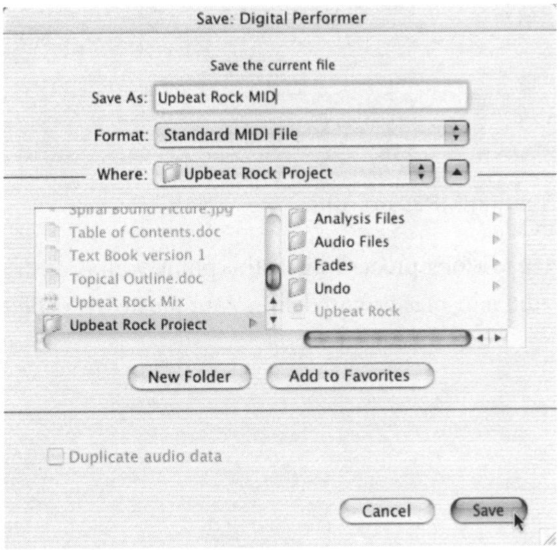

FIGURE 13.19 Saving as a Standard MIDI File

Which file you need to make will depend upon whom you are working with. Once the appropriate file is created, burn the necessary files onto a data CD.

You may also find it necessary to make MP3s. An MP3 file is a low-resolution audio file, which takes up far less computer space. MP3s are typically used when sending music as e-mail attachments or downloading music from Web sites. Their low file size allows them to transfer over the Web relatively quickly, but their low audio quality makes them unfit for many professional applications.

You can create MP3s in iTunes. First, highlight the file you wish to convert, and then choose Advanced–Convert Selection to MP3.

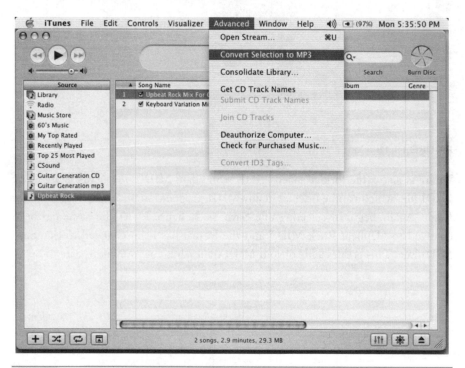

FIGURE 13.20 Creating MP3s in iTunes

This is the final step in a long process, but at this point, your project is complete. You can now record, edit, mix, master, and deliver your music with Digital Performer.

WRITING TO PICTURE

14.1 Locking to a Quicktime Movie:
Importing a Movie

It is possible to import a Quicktime Movie into your sequence, having the movie play along on your screen as you listen to the music you are writing. This can be a *very* cool thing. The Sequence Editor provides a Movie track that makes this process quite easy. To import a movie, click on "Choose" in the Track Information Panel.

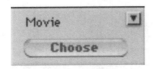

FIGURE 14.1 Track Information Panel. Movie track.

Next, locate the movie file on your hard drive, and double-click on it. This will open the file into the Sequence Editor's Movie track.

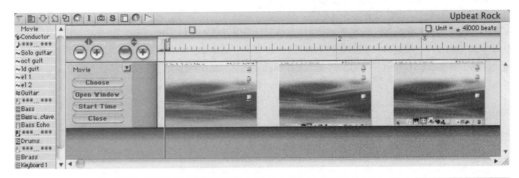

FIGURE 14.2 Movie Track

In figure 14.2, I have imported a short movie demonstrating how to open Digital Performer. The movie track will show frames of the Quicktime movie and where they fall in your sequence. It will automatically space them so that no frames overlap. This means if you zoom out, frames will be skipped.

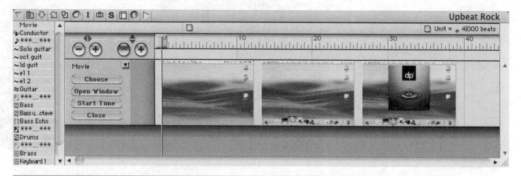

FIGURE 14.3 Movie Track. Zoomed Out.

Likewise, if you zoom in, you will see all of the individual frames, and Digital Performer will repeat frames, if necessary.

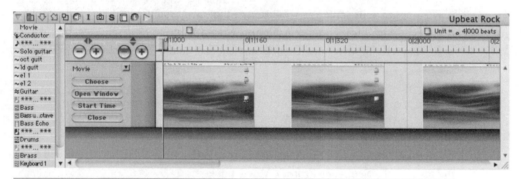

FIGURE 14.4 Movie Track. Zoomed In.

Digital Performer also has a separate window that will play back the entire movie, so that you can see the movie playing in real time along with your music. To open this window, click on "Open Window" in the Track Information Panel.

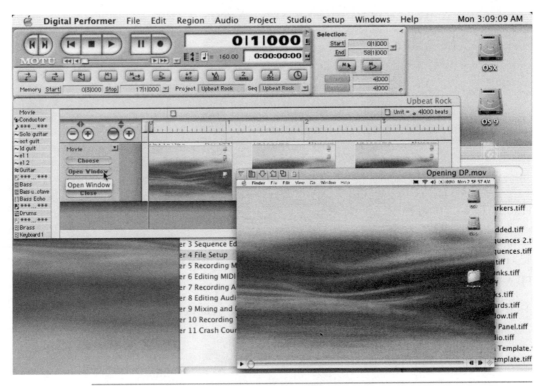

FIGURE 14.5 Movie Window

In the Movie window, there is a lock in the Title Bar. This locks the movie to the playback of the sequence, causing them to play back together. It should nearly always be on.

You can conveniently copy any audio from the movie to an audio track in your sequence. Just choose "Copy Movie Audio to Sequence" from the Movie Window mini-menu.

14.2 Start Time

If you are writing for television or film, there will most likely be visual SMPTE time code on your movie. This indicates the hour, minute, second, and frame at which your movie is starting. You can transfer this information to Digital Performer by clicking on the "Start Time" row in the movie Track Information Panel.

FIGURE 14.6 Setting the Movie Start Time

In figure 14.6, the user is setting the start time to hour 3, minute 9, second 9, frame 15. But our sequence is set to start at hour 0, meaning in won't get to hour 3 and line up with the film until measure 16,000 or so.

To rectify this, we again return to the "Start Times" in the Tempo Control drawer.

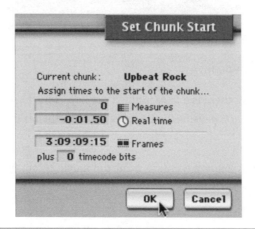

FIGURE 14.7 Setting the Sequence Start Time

In addition to setting the start time of the sequence in terms of measures and real time, we can set the start time in frames. In figure 14.7, the "frames" parameter is set to start at 3:09:09:15, the same time as the movie. Now our movie and sequence will begin together.

Of course, our sequence has a measure "zero." Ideally, we would rather have the movie start at measure 1, presumably when our music will begin. To do so, we will have to back up the start of the sequence, to account for the length of measure zero. We already know that measure zero is 1.5 seconds long, so we will back up the start time 1 second and 15 frames. (This movie runs at 30 frames per second.)

FIGURE 14.8 Setting the Sequence Start Time

Now, the movie will start exactly at measure 1, perfectly in sync with our music.

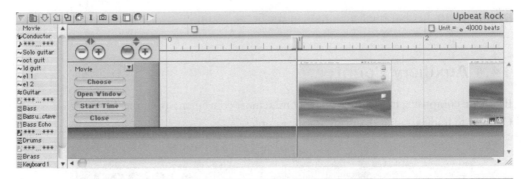

FIGURE 14.9 Movie Track

14.3 Frame Rate

The "frame rate" of the movie is the number of pictures per second. Depending on the formatting of the video, this number will vary, usually 30 fps or lower. It is important that your sequence and your Quicktime movie are set to the same frame rate, so that they will progress at the same pace. You can determine the frame rate of the Quicktime movie when you create it. You can set the frame rate of your sequence in Digital Performer's "Setup" menu.

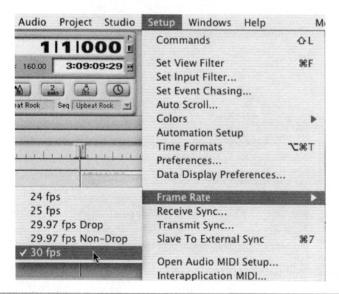

FIGURE 14.10 Setting the Frame Rate in the Setup Menu

14.4 Auxiliary Counter

If you are composing to picture, you will find it most convenient to set the Auxiliary Counter to frames, rather than real time or samples.

FIGURE 14.11 Auxiliary Counter, Set to Frames

14.5 Using Markers

Markers can be used to outline your movie, helping you write music that hits key events in the picture. Remember, markers can be created by typing Control-m. When you do so, a marker will be created at the location of the cursor. Conveniently, this also works during playback. As you watch the movie, press Control-m every time you see an event you wish to hit in order to place a marker at the hit in the Conductor track. This can be used to create a general outline of the movie.

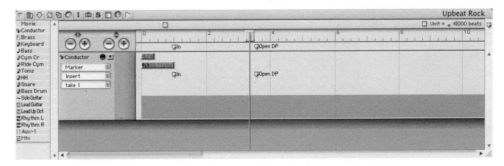

FIGURE 14.12 Conductor Track with General Markers

In figure 14.12, there is a marker at measure 1 called "In" marking the beginning of the movie. In measure 3, there is a marker call "Open DP," marking when the movie's user clicked on the Digital Performer icon in the dock.

Most likely, you will miss placing markers exactly where they should be. To place markers at the exact frame, open the Movie window. Using the step buttons ◀ ▶ at the bottom right, find the exact frame you wish to hit. This will also place the cursor at this exact point in the sequence. Now, type Control-m to create a marker.

In our case, this has resulted in the "Open DP" cursor being moved forward slightly.

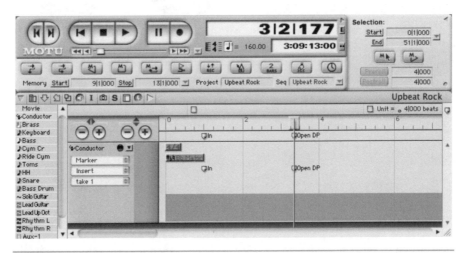

FIGURE 14.13 Exact Markers Created

Notice how the marker is located at 3:09:13:00. By default, these markers are married to their measure placement—not their timecode. This means that if we slow the tempo, the marker will remain at measure 3, beat 2, tick 177. Since the three measures will take more time to go by at a slower tempo, this placement will be later in the timecode.

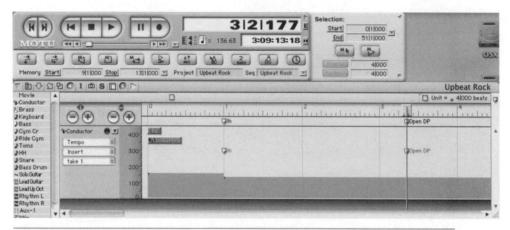

FIGURE 14.14 Tempo Change Moves Marker

Here, the tempo has been changed slightly at measure 1. While the "Open DP" marker is still at measure 3, beat 2, tick 177, it's now at 3:09:13:18. This would be a problem, since it is not where the event occurs in the movie.

You can lock markers to their respective time code, rather than their measure location. To do so, Option-click on them in the Time Ruler 🔲🕓Open DP .

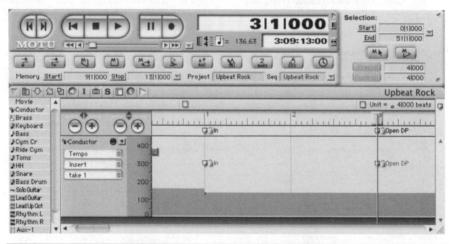

FIGURE 14.15 Markers Locked

Now, when we change tempo, the marker remains at its timecode, which originally was 3:09:13:00. The new tempo means the marker falls exactly on measure 3, beat 1, allowing us to easily hit it with a musical event.

Markers can be viewed and edited in the Markers window (shortcut: Shift-k). In figure 14.6, you can see the markers' names and locations. To change a location, click on the frame or measure, and type in a change. To view frames in the Markers window, you must open the Time Formats window in the Setup menu. Be sure to open the "Details" 🗂 tab.

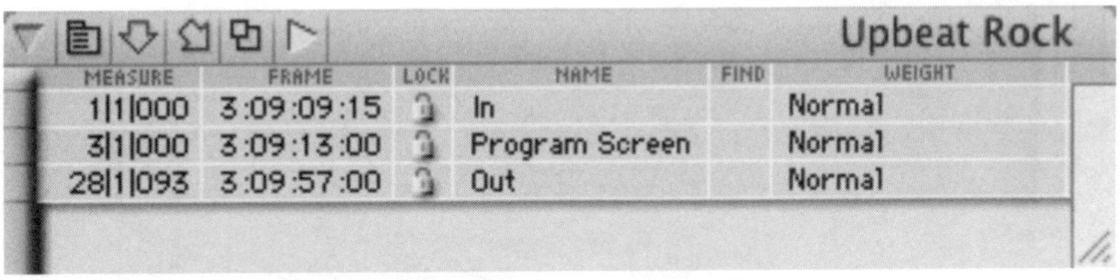

FIGURE 14.16 Markers Window

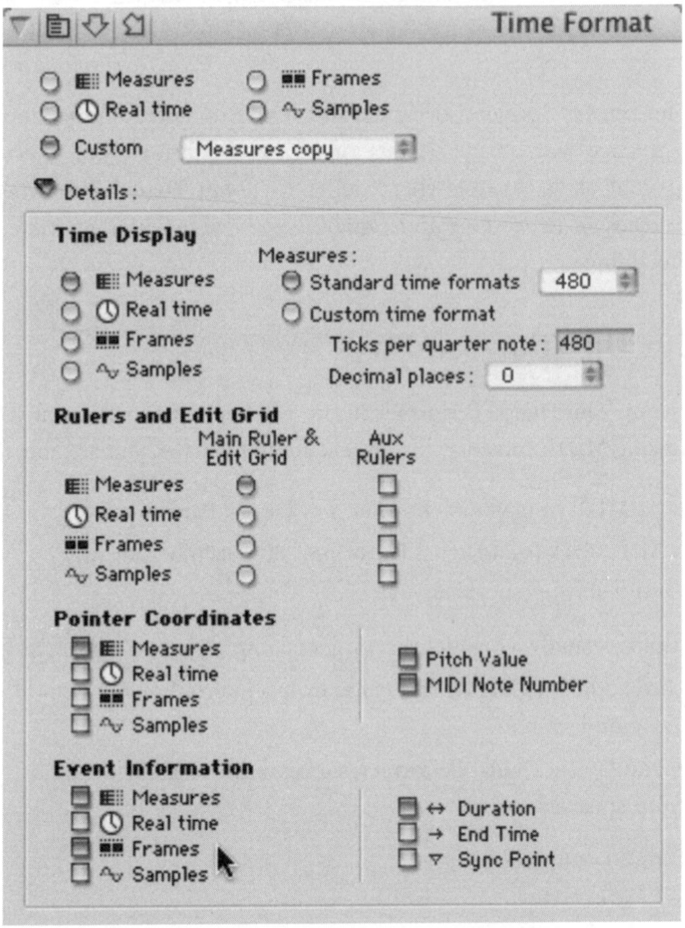

FIGURE 14.17 Time Format Window

At the bottom of figure 14.17 is an Event Information section. By turning on Frames, the Frame column will show up in the Markers Window.

Digital Performer's video capabilities are quite advanced and have made it the sequencer of choice among film scoring professionals.

DIGITAL PERFORMER PROJECTS

This chapter presents projects designed to get you up and running, and give you hands-on practice with many aspects of Digital Performer. Use these projects to develop your skills, to test what you know about Digital Performer, and to experience many of its features and capabilities. Chapter references are included with each technique.

15.1 Set Up Your Studio

How you set up your Digital Performer studio will depend on what gear you have. If you are utilizing MIDI, consider this project complete when you are able to:

1. Record MIDI from your controller into Digital Performer.
2. Play MIDI back from Digital Performer, successfully hearing the audio on your speakers.

If you are utilizing audio, consider this project complete when you are able to:

1. Record audio into Digital Performer from a microphone or your MIDI sound sources.
2. Play audio from Digital Performer, successfully hearing the audio on your speakers.

To review studio setup, see chapter 1.

15.2 Creating Tempo Changes

1. Create a new file. **SECTION 2.2**.
2. Change the Start Time of your sequence to measure 0. **SECTION 5.7**.
3. At measure 0, change the tempo of the Conductor track to 60 BPM. **SECTION 5.6**.
4. At measure 0, change the meter of the Conductor track to 3/4. **SECTION 5.6**.
5. From measure 3 to 5, gradually increase the tempo from 60 to 120. **SECTION 5.6**.

6. At measure 5, change the meter of the Conductor track to 4/4. **SECTION 5.6.**

7. Place a marker at measure 1. Call it "Intro." **SECTION 5.8.**

8. Place a marker at measure 5. Call it "A." **SECTION 5.8.**

9. Turn on the metronome, and check your tempo and meter changes. **SECTION 3.2, 3.5.**

15.3 J.S. Bach

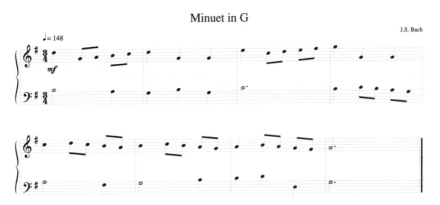

FIGURE 15.1 Bach Minuet in G

1. Create a new file. **SECTION 2.2.**

2. Change the Start Time of your sequence to measure 0. **SECTION 5.7.**

3. Select a fast tempo, and place it in the Conductor track. **SECTION 5.6.**

4. Set the Tempo Slider to a slower tempo. **SECTION 5.6.**

5. Change the meter to 3/4. **SECTION 5.6.**

6. Place a marker at measure 1. Call it "A." **SECTION 5.8.**

7. Create a MIDI track. **SECTION 5.2.**

8. Name the MIDI track "Keyboard." **SECTION 5.3.**

9. Select an appropriate output. **SECTION 5.4.**

10. Select an appropriate patch, such as a piano or harpsichord. **SECTION 5.5.**

11. Record-enable the MIDI track. **SECTION 6.1.**

12. Turn on the Metronome. **SECTION 3.5.**

13. Click Record, and perform the music. **SECTION 6.2.**

14. Quantize the music to eighth notes. Consider using a Strength percentage. **SECTION 7.10.**

15. Play back the music with the Conductor track setting the tempo. **SECTION 5.6.**

15.4 Funk Bass/Drums Groove

TRACK 15

FIGURE 15.2 Funk Bass/Drums Groove

1. Create a new file. **SECTION 2.2**.

2. Create four MIDI tracks—one each for the bass, hi-hats and cymbals, snare, and kick. **SECTION 5.2**.

3. Give each track an appropriate name. **SECTION 5.3**.

4. Give each track its own individual output. **SECTION 5.4**.

5. Select an appropriate patch for each instrument. **SECTION 5.5**.

6. Change the tempo of the Conductor track to 96 BPM. **SECTION 5.6**.

7. Change the tempo of the Tempo Slider to something slower, such as 68 BPM. **SECTION 5.6**.

8. Turn on the Metronome, and set appropriate Metronome options. **SECTION 3.5**.

9. Record each part. **SECTION 6.2**.

10. Adjust velocities and quantize. **SECTION 7.6, 7.10, 7.13**.

11. Using the Mixing Board, create a desirable mix. **SECTIONS 11.1–11.5**.

12. Take a snapshot of your mix. **SECTION 11.8**.

13. Using memory cycle, loop measures 1–4. **SECTION 3.6**.

15.5 Creating Dynamics

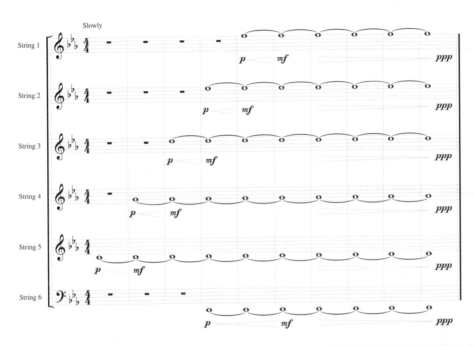

FIGURE 15.3 Dramatic Transition

1. Create a new file. **SECTION 2.2.**
2. Create the necessary MIDI tracks according to figure 15.3. **SECTION 5.2.**
3. Give each track an appropriate name. **SECTION 5.3.**
4. Give each track its own individual output. **SECTION 5.4.**
5. Assign each track an appropriate patch. **SECTION 5.5.**
6. Select an appropriate tempo, and set it in the Conductor track. **SECTION 5.6.**
7. Set the Start Time to measure 0. **SECTION 5.7.**
8. Record the "String 5" track. In the Sequence Editor, create the crescendo in measure. **SECTION 6.2, 11.9, 11.10.**
9. Record the "String 4" track. In the Mixing Board, create the crescendo in measure 2. **SECTION 6.2, 11.9, 11.10.**
10. Record the "String 3" track. In the Graphic Editor, create the crescendo in measure 3. **SECTION 6.2, 11.9, 11.10.**
11. Record the "String 2" track. Using the Region menu commands, create the crescendo in measure 4. **SECTION 6.2, 11.9, 11.10.**

12. Record the "String 1" track. In the Sequence editor or Graphic Editor, create the crescendo in measure 5 using the Expression continuous controller. Be sure also to set a "master" volume setting. **SECTION 6.2, 11.9, 11.10.**

13. Record the "String 6" track. Create the crescendo in measures 4–5 by using your favorite technique. **SECTION 6.2, 11.9, 11.10.**

14. Create the fade on one of the tracks in measures 7–10. Copy and paste this fade to all of the tracks. Be sure this does not create any sudden jumps in your Volume or Expression curves. If your setup allows you to use a Master Fader track, use a Master Fader track. **SECTION 11.9, 11.10, 11.12.**

15. Create a stereo audio track and record your mix to it. **SECTION 5.2, 9.1–9.9, 13.1.**

15.6 Poignant Moment

FIGURE 15.4 Poignant Moment

FIGURE 15.4 Poignant Moment (continued)

1. Create a new file. **SECTION 2.2.**

2. Create the necessary MIDI tracks, per figure 15.4. **SECTION 5.2.**

3. Give each track an appropriate name. **SECTION 5.3.**

4. Give each track its own, individual output. **SECTION 5.4.**

5. Assign each track an appropriate patch. **SECTION 5.5.**

6. Set the Conductor track to 60 BPM. **SECTION 5.6.**

7. If you wish, set the Tempo Slider to a slower tempo. **SECTION 5.6.**

8. Set the Start Time to measure 0. **SECTION 5.7.**

9. Change the time signature of measure 10 to 2/4. **SECTION 5.6.**

10. Record each part. Be careful; this is a transposed score. The French horn sounds a perfect fifth beneath where it is written. You can either play it a fifth lower, play it as written and transpose it afterward, or use the "Transpose" plug-in in the Mixing Board. The bass sounds an octave beneath where it is written. **SECTION 6.2, 7.12, 11.5.**

11. Using the Mixing Board, create a good mix with each instrument at full volume (forte for the strings, mezzoforte for the horn and oboe, mezzopiano for the piano). Don't forget panning. **SECTIONS 11.1–11.4.**

12. Take a snapshot of your mix. **SECTION 11.8.**

13. Play-enable the automation. **SECTION 11.8.**

14. Using continuous controller #7 or #11, create the dynamic changes (the crescendo in measure 4 and the decrescendo at the end). **SECTION 11.9, 11.10.**

15. Record your mix to a stereo audio track. **SECTIONS 9.1–9.9, 13.1.**

16. Normalize your audio file. **SECTION 13.3.**

17. Export your audio file as an AIFF. **SECTION 13.4.**

18. Burn your file onto a CD. **SECTION 13.5.**

15.7 Piano Chase Editing

P11 PIANO CHASE

1. Open "P11 Piano Chase." Assign the MIDI track to a piano patch. **SECTION 2.2, 5.5.**

2. Highlight the entire piano track, and transpose it up a minor third. **SECTION 7.12.**

3. Delete the wrong note in the chord at 31|4|000 (G#3). **SECTION 7.2.**

4. Highlight the descending scale from 2|1|000 to 3|3|240. Using Region–Change Velocity, "scale" the velocities by 50%. Listen. **SECTION 7.13.**

5. Highlight the descending scale and chord from 63|1|000 to 64|3|000. Using Region–Change Velocity, "smooth" the velocities from 100% to 30%. Listen. **SECTION 7.13.**

6. Highlight measure 75. Using Region–Change Velocity, "set" the velocities to 59. Listen. **SECTION 7.13.**

7. Highlight measure 75. Using Region–Change Velocity, "set" the velocities to 59. While doing so, "randomize" the velocities by +/–10. Listen. **SECTION 7.13.**

8. Highlight the very last note of the piece. Change its velocity to 72. Notice how this changes the voicing of the last chord. **SECTION 7.6.**

9. Highlight the entire track. Using Region–Change Velocity, "compress" the velocities. Set the threshold to 50. Set the ratio to 2:1. Listen. Section 6.10. **SECTION 7.13.**

10. Highlight the entire track. Using Region–Change Duration, "scale" the durations by 50%. Listen. **SECTION 7.11.**

11. Using the Undo History, return the sequence to where it was before you completed step 9. **SECTION 7.14.**

15.8 Knockoff

A lot can be learned by imitating music you love. For this project, recreate a piece of music from your CD collection. In this process, you will learn what you love about it: its harmonic structure, its instrumentation, its melody, and how to create similar music in your studio.

1. Select a piece of music you love.

2. Place the CD in your computer, and import the appropriate track into a sequence. **SECTION 9.9.**

3. Using the Conductor track, match the tempo of the sequence to the tempo of the audio file. **SECTION 5.6.**

4. Create the appropriate tracks for your piece, and record the parts. **SECTIONS 5.2–5.5, 6.1–6.4, 9.1–9.8.**

5. Listen to your music. What elements were you able to recreate? What elements were you not able to recreate? What can you do (such as record live guitar instead of MIDI) to improve your sequence?

15.9 Audio Editing

1. Open "P12 Audio Editing" off the CD.

2. Edit "Full Track" so that it is only 30 seconds. **SECTIONS 10.1–10.7.**

3. Edit "Full Track" so that it is only 7 seconds. **SECTIONS 10.1–10.7.**

15.10 Record Vocals

1. Open "P13 Record Vocals." Listen to the track.
2. Write some lyrics and a melody line.
3. Record your vocals over this track. **SECTIONS 9.1–9.9.**

15.11 Advanced Audio

1. Open the file "P14 Advanced Audio."
2. Create a basic mix. **SECTIONS 11.1–11.4.**
3. Place any appropriate EQs on each track. **SECTION 11.5.**
4. Create an aux track whose input is bus 3–4. **SECTION 11.6.**
5. Place a small reverb on this aux track. **SECTION 11.6.**
6. Using the sends in the mixing board, send an appropriate amount of each track to bus 3–4 (and the Aux track with the reverb). **SECTION 11.6.**
7. Create a Master Fader track that applies to the audio tracks. **SECTION 11.12.**
8. Fade out gradually, starting at measure 65. Be sure the automation is play-enabled on the Master Fader track. **SECTION 11.12.**
9. Record the mix to one stereo audio file by either:
    a. Using the "Bounce to Disk" function in the Audio Menu. **SECTION 13.2.**
    b. Sending all tracks to bus 1–2, and then recording what's on bus 1–2 on a new audio track. **SECTION 13.1.**

15.12 One Note

Create thirty seconds of music based on only one note (such as the note A). Remember all of the tricks available to you. You can use more than one octave, layer sustained patches on top of rhythmic patches, fade layered patches in and out, combine staccato patches with sustained patches, and use continuous controllers and MIDI plug-ins to shape sounds. You might record live instrumentalists, convert MIDI sounds to audio, and utilize all of your audio plug-ins. Once you can make one note interesting, just think of what you can do with your actual music.

CONCLUSION

Congratulations, you've made it! Hopefully, you've learned to record, edit, mix, and master in Digital Performer, while picking up some musical ideas along the way. Remember, despite all this technological language, ultimately, this is about bringing your musical ideas to life in the most creative and natural way possible.

I wish you all of the best with your musical projects. Thank you for reading.

Ben Newhouse
BOSTON, 2004

ABOUT THE AUTHOR

Ben Newhouse is an assistant professor at the Berklee College of Music, where he teaches music technology and production. He has worked as a music supervisor and composer on dozens of television shows, films, and Las Vegas stage shows, and for media corporations including Disney, MTV, The History Channel, A&E, Discovery, WB, NBC, ABC, FOX, and many others. Ben holds a bachelor of music in composition from the Eastman School of Music.

INDEX

A

accelerando, creating, 55, 57
AIFF format, 129
    exporting to, 190–92
Allow Measure Selection, 115
analog audio, 117
Applications menu
    Utilities
        Audio MIDI Setup, 4
Arrangement palette, 115
Arrow cursor, 108, 133
attack, 178
Attack Time controller, 167
attacks, quantizing, 90
AU plug-in format, 11, 45, 49
Audible Mode button, 25
audio bundle, 126–28
Audio Bundles window, 127–28
audio CDs, 193
audio data waveform diagrams, 30
Audio drawer, 23, 118
    Hardware button, 122
Audio Edit row, 28
audio files
    Audio Monitor window and,
        124–25
    automatic conversion of, 25
    buffer size, 121–23
    copying and pasting, 138–39
    deleting, 147–48
    editing, 132–48
    formats for, 129, 187
    inputs and outputs, 125–28
    management of, 123
    OMF and, 194
    processing, 180–82
    recording, 128–31

sample rate/format of, 117–21
sources for, 129–30
Word Clock and, 121–22
Audio Files folder, 123
    creating, 13
audio interface, 6–7, 11, 48–49,
    119–20, 121
Audio menu, 180–81
    apply spectral effects, 182
    Bounce to Disk, 186
    Fade, 143, 144
    Normalize, 189
Audio Monitor window, 124–25, 184
Audio side panel, 119, 120, 130–31
audio tracks, 26
    assigning outputs, 47
    automating panning on, 174–75
    creating, 43
    creating dynamics on, 172
    cursors for, 133–36
    information panel, 27–29
    inserts for, 153–56
    recording, 117–31
audio voices, 28, 130–31
Audio Volume data, 172
Auto Repeat, 22
Auto Rewind, 22
Auto Scroll, 25
Auto Stop, 22
Automatic Conversion button, 25,
    129–30
Automatic Snapshot button, 25, 163
Automatic Snapshot window, 164–65
automation
    continuous controllers compared
        with, 167
    controlling from Sequence Editor, 28

MIDI, 174
    play-enabling, 166, 172
    snapshot of, 25
Automation Play button, 166
Aux tracks. *See* auxiliary tracks
Auxiliary Counter, 19, 202
auxiliary tracks, 26
    adding, 44
    assigning inputs, 48–49
    naming, 127
    using busses with, 158–59
Available column, 124

B

Begin playback, 18
Begin recording, 18
bit depth. *See* sample rate
Bounce to Disk window, 186–87
bouncing to disk, 185–86
Brightness controller, 167, 174
buffer size, 121–22
burning to CD, 192–94
busses, 157–60, 184
Bypass button, 154

C

cables
    ADAT Lightpipe, 5
    quarter-inch, 5
    S/PDIF, 5, 183
    serial, 3, 11
    TDIF, 5
CDs, burning, 6, 192–94
Change Duration menu, 97–98
Change Tempo window, 54–55
Change Velocities window, 100
channels, 47

Channels popup, 187
Close Box button, 24
Collapse button, 25
Compact command, 147–48
composite performance, creating, 145–46
Compress command, 100–101
compression, 189, 190
Conductor Track, 25, 43, 53–58
    changing, 54–57
    editing markers in, 61
    meter and key changes in, 58
    Tempo Indicator in, 20
    Tempo Slider compared with, 53, 57–58
Configure Hardware Driver window, 122
constructive editing, 181
continuous controllers, 166–67
    editing from Graphic Editor, 106
    using, 168–72
Control Panel, 14, 18–23
    Click & Countoff Options window, 21
    counters, 19–20
    drawers, 23, 53, 57, 83–85, 103–4, 118, 200
    Memory Cycle, 22
    Metronome, Countoff, and Wait features, 20–21
    Overdub feature, 67
    Playback Control, 18–19
    Punch-In feature, 67–68
    Tempo Indicator, 20
Convert Sample Format, 119
Convert Sample Rate, 119
Copy function, 87–88, 134, 138–39
counters, 19–20
Countoff function, 21
CPU load, busses and, 159–60
Create Continuous Data menu, 171
Create Fades window, 140–42
crescendo, creating, 140
Cross-hair cursor, 71–72, 78, 108, 133–34, 137, 138, 139, 143
crossfades, 143–45, 146
Custom Type window, 162
Cut function, 87–88
cutdowns, 138

D
data CDs, 194
Data Type property, 73
Data types (automation snapshot), 165
decay, 178
deleting notes, 71–73
deleting unused audio, 147–48
destructive editing, 189
digital audio, 117
Digital Performer. *See also specific features and topics*
    audio file/hardware discrepancies noted in, 119–20
    audio interface used with, 6–7
    basics, 12–17
    Control Panel in, 18–23
    editing audio in, 132–48
    editing MIDI in, 70–102
    editing windows in, 103–16
    environment, 14
    external effects used with, 8
    file management in, 123
    file setup in, 37–62
    file structure, 12–13
    hint labels in, 28–29
    installing, 1
    internal mixing board, 10, 50, 149–76
    launching, 13
    microphone used with, 7–8
    mixing board used with, 5–6
    musical considerations in, 177–82
    printing a final mix in, 183–96
    project backup, 13
    projects, 206–14
    Reason used with, 50–51
    recording a mix in, 183–96
    recording audio in, 117–31
    recording MIDI in, 63–69
    Sequence Editor in, 24–36
    setup, 1–11
    software plug-ins used with, 11
    using MIDI with, 3–4
    writing to picture in, 197–205
Digital Performer menu
    Preferences, 58
Digital Performer User Guide, 122
Digital Word Clock, 121–22
Drum Editor, 104, 108–11

Duration, 73
dynamics, 189
    creating, 168–71, 172
Dynamics palette, 115

E
"ear candy," 180
Echo insert, 153–54, 156, 158–59
Echo plug-in window, 153–54
Edit menu
    Copy, 88
    Deselect, 85
    Merge, 88
    Paste, 88
    Repeat, 88–89
    Select All, 85
    Snip, 138
    Split, 139
    Undo History, 101
Edit Resolution button, 69, 72–73, 74–75, 76, 107
effects, outboard, 156
effects plug-ins, 152, 153–57
    CPU load and, 160
    using busses with, 158–59
Emphasis feature, 93
end point, changing, 74–75
EQ, 152
    automating, 175–76
    setting, 154–56, 182
Equal gain, 144
Equal power, 144
Event Information Bar, 73–74, 77, 89, 107
Event List Editor, 104
Event List window, 91–92, 104, 166–67
eVerb plug-in, 160
Expand button, 25, 32, 107, 114
Expand feature, 149
Expression controller, 167, 171–72
Extend Releases option, 98

F
fade-ins, 140–43, 190
fade-outs, 140–43, 190
fades, 140–45, 163
Fall Behind button, 25
file delivery formats, 192–96
file format, 15

File menu
    New, 13, 16, 37
    Save, 15
    Save As, 15, 194, 195
    Save As Template, 15
file size, sample rate/format and, 118
Finale software program, 195
Finger cursor, 87, 134
FireWire cable, 3, 6, 10, 11
Flush command, 102
frame rate, 201–2
Frames parameter, 200

G

gain, 101
Graphic Editor, 104, 105–8
Grid setting, 91
Groove Quantize window, 95–96
Groove Quantizing, 94–96, 111
grooves, creating, 96–97
grouping tracks, 161–62

H

Hand cursor, 32, 74–75, 108
Hardware button, 122
Harmonize command, 99
Humanizing, 111

I

I-Beam tool, 70, 81–83, 86, 87, 88,
    135, 137, 139, 143, 189
Import popup, 187
IN number column, 125
Independent feature, 144
input (of track), 28, 125–28
input signal, 154
Insert button, 130
Insert Loop tool, 71
Insert Soundbite button, 25
Instrument track, 26, 49
interleaved-stereo file, 191
internal bussing, 157–60
iTunes window, 193, 196

K

key, changing, 58
Korg
    sound modules, playback modes
      on, 53

Triton MIDI controller, 3, 10
Triton Rack, 3, 4, 5, 48–49, 64

L

Lasso cursor, 80, 86
latency, 121
layering tracks, 179–80
Legato Pedal controller, 167
Level column, 124–25
Lightning Bolt icon, 129
Limit command, 100
Location, 73
Logic software program, 116, 195
Loop tool, 89
loops, creating, 88–90

M

MachFive, 49
Main Counter, 19
Main Out audio bundle, reassigning,
    128
markers, 60–61, 202–5
Markers window, 204–5
Marquee tool, 70
    object selection with, 86
    shape changes, 71–72, 80
MAS plug-in format, 11, 49
Master Device, 122
Master Fader track, 26, 173
mastering, 189–90
Measures Counter, 19
Memory Cycle settings, 22
Memory Play feature, 23, 84–85
Merge function, 87–88
meter, changing, 58
Metronome, 20–21
microphones, connecting, 7–8, 125
MIDI, 1–2
    Audible Mode button and, 25
    audio setup, 4, 9
    automating, 174
    connections, 2–3
    data representation, 30
    editing, 70–102
    mixing board setup, 5–6
    orchestrating, 177–79
    recording, 63–69
MIDI controllers, 2–3, 11
    signal flow through, 9

MIDI Edit row, 29
MIDI files
    OMF and, 194
    SMF, 195
MIDI In port, 1, 2–3
MIDI interface, 3–4, 11
    signal flow through, 9
MIDI messages, 1–2, 163
    metronome clicks, 21
    Wait function and, 21
MIDI Out port, 1, 2–3
MIDI Thru port, 1, 2–3
MIDI tracks, 25
    assigning outputs, 47, 49
    converting to audio, 151, 156
    creating, 42–43
    information panel, 29
    inserts for, 156–57
    layering, 178, 179–80
Mini-Menu button, 24–25
Mix percentage, 154
mixing, creating a basic, 151–52
mixing board
    combining tracks through, 183
    connecting to, 28
    digital, 121
    function of, 49–50
    setup, 5–6
    signal flow through, 9
    track output assignments, 46
Mixing Board window, 10, 14, 50,
    149–76
    combining tracks through, 183–84
    layout, 149
    Record-Enable button in, 63, 168,
      175–76
    setting panning in, 150–51
    setting volumes in, 150
    Snapshot icon in, 163–64
Modulation controller, 167, 174
MOTU 828 Mark II, 6–7, 9–10, 121,
    125
MOTU Micro Express, 3
MOTU products technical support, 1
Move cursor, 33
Move Releases option, 97–98
Movie track, 26, 43, 197–99
Movie window, 198–99
    mini-menu, 199

step buttons, 203
movies, importing, 197–99
moving notes, 71–73
MP3 format, 129, 195–96
Multimode Filter, 182
Mute button, 110, 157
Mute Soundbite tool, 71
MW Compressor, 190

N

New File Template, 13, 14, 16
non-destructive editing, 146–47
normalizing a mix, 189–90
Notation Editor, 111–13
Note layer, 76
Note Name, 73
Note Off message, 2
Note On message, 1–2, 21, 59
notes
    deleting and moving, 71–73
    quantizing, 90–97

O

object selection, 86
Off-Velocity, 73
Offset feature, 110
OMF Interchange file format, 194–95
On-Velocity, 73
Open File dialog box, 13
orchestrating with MIDI, 177–79
OSX System Preferences, 21
output (of track), 28, 125–28
Overdub button, 67
overdubbing, 67, 69

P

Pan controller, 167
panning
    automating, 174, 175
    setting, 150–51, 152, 163
Paste function, 87–88, 134, 138–39
Patch Selection, 29, 52
patches, 2–3
    assigning, 52–53
    default settings, 52
Pause playback, 18
PCM80, 156
Pencil icon, 107–8
Pencil tool, 56–57, 69, 71, 170, 174, 176

Percentage option, 93, 96
Piano Keyboard icon, 30
Pitch Bend controller, 106, 174
Pitch Ruler, 87, 106, 108, 116
Play-Enable button, 27, 110, 168, 175
playback control, 18–19
playlists, 193
plug-ins, 11
    assigning tracks, 49–51
    creating tracks, 44–45
    formats of, 11
Portamento Time controller, 167
Postroll parameter, 23, 85
preamps, 7, 125
Preroll parameter, 23, 85
Pro Tools software program, 116, 194
processed signal, 154
Project Folder, 12–13
    creating, 13, 37
    reducing size of, 102
Project menu
    Add Track
        Aux Track, 44
        Instrument Track, 45
        Master Fader, 173
        MIDI Track, 42–43
        Mono Audio Track, 43
    Delete Tracks, 44
    Modify Conductor Track, 58
        Change Tempo, 54
    Modify Track Groups
        New Track Group, 161
    opening Sequence Editor from, 26
Punch-In menu, 68
Punch-In recording, 67–68

Q

quantize, 90–97
    in Drum Editor, 110–11
Quantize window, 90–91
Quick Filter, 34–36, 56
Quickscribe Editor, 104, 113–15
    mini-menu, 114–15
    toolbar features, 114
Quicktime movies, 197–99, 201–2

R

Randomize function, 93
ratio, 101

Real Time Counter, 19, 60
Reason software program, 50–51, 125, 195
Record button, 168
Record-Enable button, 27, 63–64
recording a mix, 183–96
Region menu
    Change Duration, 97
    Create Continuous Data, 170–71
    Create Groove, 96–97
    Groove Quantize, 94–95
    Quantize, 90–91
    Set Loop, 90
    Transpose, 99, 182
    velocity change in, 99–100
Release Time controller, 167
removing space, 136–38
Reshape Flavor tool, 57, 71, 170, 174
Reshape Mode tool, 71
Reshape tool, 71
Resize button, 25
Return key, moving insertion point
    with, 82
reverb, 152, 156, 160
Rewind, 18–19, 65–66
Rewire plug-in format, 11, 49, 50
Rhythm Brush tool, 71
ritard, creating, 55
Roland
    A-30, 3
    sound modules, playback modes
        on, 53
    XV-3080, 3, 4, 5, 21, 47, 48–49,
        150, 163

S

S/PDIF cable, 5, 183
sample format, 118–21
sample rate, 117–19
    choosing, 187
    setting, 122
samplers, 3, 11
    velocity and, 77
Samples Counter, 19
sampling libraries, 177
Scale feature, 100
Scissors tool, 71, 75–76, 135–36, 139,
    146
Score Options, 115

Scrub tool, 71
SDII format. *See* Sound Designer II (SDII) format
Select All feature, 85, 87
selecting data, 78–87
Selection drawer, 23, 83–85
Selection mini-menu, 83–84
send knobs, 157–58
Sensitivity feature, 94
Sequence Editor, 14, 24–36
  automating panning from, 174
  Automation Snapshot and, 165–66
  changing start time in, 59–60
  choosing plug-ins in, 181
  compared with other editing windows, 116
  Conductor track changed from, 55
  controller data viewed in, 168–69
  default tracks in, 37
  durations in, 30
  Event Information Bar and, 74
  example layouts for, 34–36
  Graphic Editor and, 105
  Insert feature, 58
  markers in, 60–61
  Memory Play and, 84–85
  MIDI track structure, 30
  mini-menu, 16–17, 31, 103
  Movie track, 197
  Quick Filter in, 34–36
  Record-Enable button in, 63
  Title Bar buttons, 24–25, 130
  Track Information panel, 26–29, 32–33
  track manipulation in, 31–33
  track types in, 25–26
  tracks in, 43–45
  tracks overview, 29–30
  volume editing in, 169–70
  Zoom
    Set Zoom Setting, 31
    Zoom Back, 31
    Zoom Forward, 31
Sequence File, 13
sequencers, 2, 11
sequences, multiple, 16–17
serial cable, 3, 11
Set command, 100
Setup menu

Configure Audio System
  Configure Hardware Driver, 6–7
Open Audio MIDI Setup, 4
Open Time Format window, 204–5
setting frame rate in, 201–2
shortcuts
  Command-[(zoom back), 31
  Command-] (zoom forward), 31
  Command-0 (quantize), 90
  Command-8 (open Step Record), 68
  Command-9 (transpose), 99
  Command-a (select all), 17, 85
  Command arrows (zoom features), 31, 106, 109
  Command-c (copy), 88
  Command-click (hides indicated track), 32
  Command-d (deselect), 85
  Command-m (merge), 88
  Command-n (create new file), 13, 16
  Command-o (open file), 13
  Command-r (repeat), 88–89
  Command-s (save file), 15
  Command-v (paste), 88
  Control-arrows (patch selection), 52
  Control-Command-a (add aux track), 44
  Control-f (open Create Fades window), 140–42, 144
  Control-m (create marker), 61, 202, 203
  decimal key (cycle counter fields), 20
  double-clicking on data, 78–79, 87, 108
  double-clicking on keyboard icon, 79–80, 87
  double-clicking on send knob, 157
  down arrow (sends record-enable button down), 64
  for editing tools, 70–71
  keyboard (for memory cycle), 22
  keyboard (for playback control), 19
  numeric keypad (for metronome), 22
  numeric keypad (for playback control), 22

Option-arrows (available channels), 47
Option-click (bypass), 154
Option-click (hides tracks), 32
Option-click (name tracks), 45
Option-clicking on send knob, 157
Option key, holding down, 44
Option-Shift-Command-a (add multiple audio tracks), 44
Option-Shift-Command-m (add multiple MIDI tracks), 44
Shift-a (open audio monitor), 124
Shift-arrows (MIDI output changes), 47
Shift-b (open Soundbites window), 119, 132
Shift-Command-a (create audio tracks), 43
Shift-Command-m (create MIDI tracks), 42
Shift-k (edit markers), 204
Shift-m (Mixing Board), 14, 149
Shift-o (Tools Palette), 70, 170
Shift-s (Sequence Editor), 14, 26
Shift-u (open Audio Bundles window), 127
Shift-x (Control Panel), 14
up arrow (sends record-enable button up), 64
Show/Hide Track Information button, 109
signal flow, 9
Skip forwards or backwards, 18–19
SMF file format, 195
Smooth command, 101
SMPTE time code, 199–200
Snapshot icon, 163–64
Snip editing function, 137–38
Soft Pedal controller, 167
software sound sources. *See* plug-ins
Solo button, 25
Sostenuto controller, 167
Sound Designer II (SDII) format, 129, 190–92
sound modules, 2, 3, 11, 177–79
  assigning outputs, 47, 48–49
  continuous controllers and, 167
  playback modes, 53
  reverb and, 156

signal flow through, 9
volume setting on, 163
soundbites, 28, 132
editing, 133–48
quantizing, 90–97
Soundbites window, 119–20, 132–33
adding to, 187–88
Edit mode, 189–90
Info mode, 189
inserting audio from, 25
List mode, 189
mini-menu, 119, 147–48, 191
spectral effects, 182
start point, changing, 74–75
start time, setting, 199–201
Step buttons, 203
Step-Record window, 68
step recording, 68
stereo bundle, 126
stereo files, importing, 130
Stop playback, 18
Strength feature, 94, 111
Studio Configuration window, 130
Studio menu
Audio Monitor, 124
Step-Record window, 68
Time Formats, 74
Tools, 70
submixes, 161–62, 185–86
Sustain Pedal controller, 167
Swing feature, 91, 92–93, 111
synthesizers, 3, 11

T
Tab key, moving insertion point with,
82
Take feature, 28, 146
Take File column, 124
Take Folder column, 124
templates, 15–16
tempo, setting, 53–59
Tempo Control drawer, 23, 53, 57
Start Times button, 59–60, 200
tempo curve types, 55
Tempo Indicator, 20
Tempo Slider, 20
changing, 57
Conductor Track compared with,
53, 57–58

recording MIDI with, 64, 69
threshold, 101
ticks, 19
Time Code Counter, 19, 204
Time Format window, 74, 204–5
Time Range (automation snapshot),
164–65
time-range selection, 86, 88
Time Ruler, 30, 56, 204
selecting data with, 82–83, 87
timeline, 108
Title Bar buttons, 24–25, 199
Tools Palette, 14, 70–71, 170. See also
specific tools
Track Edit window
Record-Enable button in, 63
track groups, 161–62
track height, changing, 32
Track Information panel, 26–29, 52
audio track information, 27–29
Auto row, 166
changing conductor track, 55–57
changing track height in, 32
Continuous Data Mode, 168–69
data view preferences, 168–69
in Drum Editor, 109–10
Insert
Controller, 170, 174
layers viewed in, 76–77
MIDI track information, 29
Open Window, 198
reordering tracks in, 33
Start Time row, 199–200
Take feature, 146
Track Options, 115
Track Selector section, 107–8
Track Settings menu, 27
Track Type icon, 27
tracks
assigning outputs, 46–52
creating, 42–45
naming, 45–46, 107, 127
Tracks (automation snapshot), 165
Tracks Overview, 26, 29–30
Tracks window, 115–16
Transpose command, 99
Transpose window, 99
Transposition option, 115
transposition plug-ins, 156–57

Trimmer cursor, 134, 136–37
Tuplet feature, 91

U
Undo History window, 101–2
mini-menu, 102
Unit parameter, 72–73, 74–75
Unit Resolution, 112–13
"Upbeat Rock" example, 37–42
USB, 3, 11

V
velocity
changing, 99–101
editing from Graphic Editor, 106
Velocity layer, 76–77
virtual instruments. See plug-ins
volume, velocity compared with, 77
Volume controller, 106, 167
creating dynamics with, 168–71
Expression compared with, 171–72
Volume Fader, 150, 163
volumes, setting, 150, 151–52, 163

W
Wait function, 21
WAV format, 129
Windows drawer, 23, 103–4
opening Sequence Editor from, 26
Windows menu, 119

Y
Yamaha 02R, 121

Z
Zoom buttons, 31, 106
Zoom feature, 30, 197–98
Zoom tool, 71, 106, 109

NOTES

NOTES

NOTES

NOTES

NOTES

NOTES

NOTES

Berklee Press DVDs:
Just Press PLAY

AS SERIOUS ABOUT MUSIC AS YOU ARE

**Kenwood Dennard:
The Studio/ Touring Drummer**

| ISBN: 0-87639-022-X | HL: 50448034 | DVD $19.95 |

**Up Close with Patti Austin: Auditioning
and Making it in the Music Business**

| ISBN: 0-87639-041-6 | HL: 50448031 | DVD $19.95 |

**The Ultimate Practice
Guide for Vocalists**

| ISBN: 0-87639-035-1 | HL: 50448017 | DVD $19.95 |

Featuring Donna McElroy

**Real-Life Career Guide for the
Professional Musician**

| ISBN: 0-87639-031-9 | HL: 50448013 | DVD $19.95 |

Featuring David Rosenthal

Essential Rock Grooves for Bass

| ISBN: 0-87639-037-8 | HL: 50448019 | DVD $19.95 |

Featuring Danny Morris

Jazz Guitar Techniques: Modal Voicings

| ISBN: 0-87639-034-3 | HL: 50448016 | DVD $19.95 |

Featuring Rick Peckham

Jim Kelly's Guitar Workshop

| ISBN: 0-634-00865-X | HL: 00320168 | DVD $19.95 |

**Basic Afro-Cuban Rhythms for
Drum Set and Hand Percussion**

| ISBN: 0-87639-030-0 | HL: 50448012 | DVD $19.95 |

Featuring Ricardo Monzón

**Vocal Technique: Developing
Your Voice for Performance**

| ISBN: 0-87639-026-2 | HL: 50448038 | DVD $19.95 |

Featuring Anne Peckham

Preparing for Your Concert

| ISBN: 0-87639-036-X | HL: 50448018 | DVD $19.95 |

Featuring JoAnne Brackeen

**Jazz Improvisation: Starting Out with
Motivic Development**

| ISBN: 0-87639-032-7 | HL: 50448014 | DVD $19.95 |

Featuring Ed Tomassi

Chop Builder for Rock Guitar

| ISBN: 0-87639-033-5 | HL: 50448015 | DVD $19.95 |

Featuring "Shred Lord" Joe Stump

Turntable Technique: The Art of the DJ

| ISBN: 0-87639-038-6 | HL: 50448025 | DVD $24.95 |

Featuring Stephen Webber

**Jazz Improvisation: A Personal
Approach with Joe Lovano**

| ISBN: 0-87639-021-1 | HL: 50448033 | DVD $19.95 |

Harmonic Ear Training

| ISBN: 0-87639-027-0 | HL: 50448039 | DVD $19.95 |

Featuring Roberta Radley